WEB
Commerce

Upside Books examines events in business and management through the lens of technology. *Upside Magazine* is the preeminent magazine for executives and managers eager to understand the business of high tech.

PUBLISHED:

High Tech, High Hope: Turning Your Vision of Technology into Business Success, Paul Franson

Risky Business: Protect Your Business from Being Stalked, Conned, or Blackmailed on the Web, Daniel S. Janal

Web Commerce: Building a Digital Business, Kate Maddox

Managing Telework: Strategies for Managing the Virtual Workforce, Jack M. Nilles

FORTHCOMING:

Silicon Gold Rush: The Next Generation of High-Tech Stars Rewrite the Rules of Business, Karen Southwick

Web
Commerce

Building a
Digital Business

KATE MADDOX

with Dana Blankenhorn

John Wiley & Sons, Inc.

New York • Chichester • Weinheim • Brisbane • Singapore • Toronto

Published by John Wiley & Sons, Inc.
Published simultaneously in Canada.

This publication is designed to provide accurate and authoritative information in
regard to the subject matter covered. It is sold with the understanding that the
publisher is not engaged in rendering professional services. If professional advice
or other expert assistance is required, the services of a competent professional
person should be sought.

Library of Congress Cataloging-in-Publication Data:

Maddox, Kate, 1961–
    Web commerce : building a digital business / Kate Maddox with
Dana Blankenhorn.
        p.   cm.
    Includes index.
    ISBN 0-471-29282-6 (cloth : alk. paper)
    1. Electronic commerce.   2. Business enterprises—Computer
networks.   3. World Wide Web (Information retrieval system)
I. Blankenhorn, Dana.   II. Title.
HF5548.32.M33   1998
658.8′00285′4678—dc21   98-13347

Printed in the United States of America.

10 9 8 7 6 5 4 3 2

Preface

This book is designed to help you identify the different solutions for Web commerce and find a system that works best for your business. It's also designed to help you develop strategies for making your site successful, whether you're a large or small company.

■ PART I THE WEB: A NEW BUSINESS MODEL

Chapter 1 provides an overview of Web commerce, including current revenue figures and projections. In Chapter 2, we look at how Horizon Tours, a small travel agency, built a Web commerce business using AT&T's Secure Buy hosting service, costing about $700 a month. And in Chapter 3, we examine how Cisco Systems spent millions to build an in-house system that is now generating close to $4 billion a year in business-to-business sales.

While these two case studies are very different, there are some similarities that apply to every business, big or small. In each, the business executives charged with creating the Web commerce operations needed to develop a strategy for selling on the Web, evaluate different system solutions, build the systems, and promote them. There are lessons to be learned from each case study.

■ PART II   PUTTING THE PIECES TOGETHER

The chapters in Part II take an in-depth look at some of the major categories of software and systems for transacting Web commerce. Each chapter in this part will look at the features, pricing, setup requirements, and pros and cons of each type of system, and describe what types of businesses these solutions are best suited for. In addition, each chapter includes at least one case study of a business that has implemented the system, and discusses what kind of success it is having with it as well as any problems.

This book takes a very comprehensive look at most of the leading solutions for Web commerce available today and will help you decide which system may be right for your business. The case studies describe in detail what's required to set up the system, from both a cost and resource standpoint. The final chapter in this part, on security, takes a look at one of the most pressing and important issues surrounding Web commerce, and what's being done to resolve it.

■ PART III   INDUSTRY APPLICATIONS

Beyond selecting the right kinds of hardware, software, payment options, and security solutions for your Web commerce system, there are also issues to consider that go beyond system setup. Depending on what kind of industry you're in or what kind of customers you have, you'll want to develop unique strategies to make the most of your Web commerce systems. If you're a car manufacturer, what are some of the problems you'll face trying to sell expensive items over the Web? If you are a business-to-business seller, how do you avoid disrupting the sales channel? The chapters in Part III address industry-specific questions and present strategies for dealing with them.

■ PART IV CASHING IN ON WEB COMMERCE

Once you've put the major systems in place for your Web commerce business, it's time to start seeing some results. The chapters in Part IV will look at technologies and strategies to help you reach your target audience, such as personalization and promotion of your site. Chapter 15 examines some of the impacts of Web commerce on the marketplace. Finally, Chapter 16 looks into the future of Web commerce.

■ METHODOLOGY

In conducting research for this book, the authors interviewed more than 100 sources, including executives in Information Systems (IS) and business operations at companies now engaging in successful Web commerce; presidents, CEOs, electronic commerce strategists, product line managers, marketing managers, and other executives at dozens of software and hardware companies now providing solutions for electronic commerce; systems integrators, consultants, Web developers, and other third parties that provide Web solutions; and researchers, analysts, and other industry watchers, for a broader perspective. Most of these interviews were conducted on-site and in some cases over a period of several days. Because Web commerce is such a broad market made up of thousands of providers, many important players were not included in this book. A partial list of sources includes:

Actra Business Systems (now Netscape): Ray Rike, vice president, marketing and sales

American Financial and Investment Inc.: Jack Rodgers, president

AT&T: Keith Olson, director, new channel development

Auto-By-Tel: John Markovich, chief financial officer

BroadVision Inc.: Sandra Vaughan, senior director, corporate marketing

BSG: Morgan Pierce, managing director

CerfNet: Push Mohta, executive vice president

Cisco Systems Inc.: Chris Sinton, senior manager, Cisco Connection; Susan Aragon, IS manager, electronic commerce; Todd Elizalde, senior manager, electronic commerce

CommerceNet: Randall Whiting, president; Stacy Bressler, vice president, marketing

Connect Inc.: Pam Kostka, director, product marketing

CyberCash Inc.: Teresa Crummett, director, corporate marketing

CyberSource: Bill McKiernan, president

DoubleClick: Kevin O'Connor, president

Fingerhut: Jane Westlind, manager, electronic commerce

First Virtual Holdings: Pierre Wolff, director, strategy

Global Interactive Systems: Jason Heffran, vice president, electronic commerce

Guthy-Renker Internet: Kenneth Burke, vice president, development

Hewlett-Packard Co.: Gary O'Neall, general manager, electronic commerce

Horizon Tours: Dimple Morrow, owner; Eddie Lloyd, regional sales director

IBM Corp.: Tom Patterson, chief strategist, electronic commerce

ICAT: Craig Danuloff, president and CEO

Internet Factory: John Murray, vice president, marketing

Intershop: Stephan Schambach, president and CEO

Interworld Technology Ventures Inc.: Robert Zangrillo, co-founder, chairman, and CEO; Michael Donahue, president and chief technology officer

KPMG: Robin Palmer, partner in charge, electronic commerce; Bob Buce, partner in charge, compensation and benefits; Brian Kirk, senior manager, information, communications, and entertainment

MCI: David Samuels, product manager, Web Commerce

Microsoft Corp.: Gytis Barzdukas, product manager, Internet commerce marketing

Modem Media-Poppe Tyson: Art Melville, group account director

Multimedia Resource Group: John Audette, founder

NECX: Henry Bertolon, president and CEO; Judy Ashley, MIS director; Brian Marley, general manager, direct channels

Open Market Inc.: Wendy Ziner, director, marketing communications

Procure.Net: Bob Grzyb, vice president, marketing

RSA Data Security: Scott Schnell, vice president, marketing

Security Dynamics: Dave Power, vice president, marketing and corporate development

Square Earth: Brad Galle, chief executive officer

UUNet: Paul Hoffman, manager, Web product marketing and development

VeriSign Inc.: Anil Pereira, director, consumer and corporate marketing; Bob Pratt, product line manager

Yoyodyne Corp.: Seth Godin, president

KATE MADDOX

Acknowledgments

This book was accomplished with the help of many people. First, I would like to thank Noah Shachtman, former acquisitions editor at Van Nostrand Reinhold (which was merged with John Wiley & Sons, Inc. in late 1997), who proposed this book idea to me in early 1997. I would also like to thank Jeanne Glasser, business editor at Wiley, who brought *Web Commerce* to fruition, and the editors at Publications Development Company of Texas, who incorporated the many updates and produced the book. *Web Commerce* would not have been possible without the hard work of my colleague Dana Blankenhorn, who helped me complete this project when I took a new position at *Advertising Age* midway through the writing of this book.

My experience in this field is due largely to the support of my editor and mentor for the past decade, David Klein, associate publisher/editor of *Advertising Age,* and former editor-in-chief of CMP Media's *Interactive Age,* a start-up publication covering electronic commerce when the industry was in its infancy. I would also like to thank the many talented editors with whom I've worked through the years at Crain Communications' *Electronic Media, Advertising Age* and *Business Marketing* publications, and CMP's *Interactive Age, CommunicationsWeek* (now *InternetWeek*), and *InformationWeek*. Many, many executives in the electronic commerce industry spent valuable hours sharing their stories and wisdom with us, and I would like to extend my appreciation to them. A list of the key sources for this book is provided on pages vii through ix. Their willingness to talk about their experiences in Web commerce will help readers identify the challenges and solutions to making this a viable business.

I would also like to acknowledge the love and encouragement of my parents, David and Martha Oberlander, who have given me the strength to realize my dreams. And finally, I owe this book to the love and support of my husband, Sam, and children, Max and Madeline, who endured hours and hours of Mom's being locked away in her office while writing *Web Commerce*.

K.M.

I want to acknowledge David Klein, who gave me this beat and *NetMarketing* editor, Karen Egolf, who kept me on it. I also want to acknowledge the entire launch team of *Interactive Age* for their great work in showing how this beat should be covered.

Finally, I want to thank my wife, Jenni, who has actually been *doing* electronic commerce for 15 years. She taught me this very complex business, while supporting my efforts to cover it, and giving me my two best reasons for looking forward to the twenty-first century—Robin and John.

D.B.

Contents

Introduction

At Spring Internet World 97 in Los Angeles, I met a business executive in the Open Market booth, where he was being shown a demo of a system to conduct secure electronic transactions over the Internet. He spent about forty-five minutes with the eager sales representative, scratching his chin and squinting at the computer screen as he studied the graphical user interfaces (GUIs) and order management setup procedures. After the demo was over, he started to wander away, scanning the 600,000-square-foot exhibit floor at the Los Angeles Convention Center and probably wondering which of the 600-plus exhibitors to hit next. I intercepted him and started asking him questions about what he was looking for in a commerce system, what his goals were, and which systems he was looking at, and he told me that he was just starting to shop around for electronic commerce software to automate his business, which deals in energy trading.

This was his biggest frustration, and it's true for most businesspeople who want to set up shop on the Web: trying to figure out what all of these electronic commerce companies do, and how to fit the different pieces together to build the right kind of e-commerce system. For companies just starting out in this field, and even for those that have been at it for a while, it can be overwhelming to try to understand the differences between VeriSign and VeriFone, CyberCash and CyberSource, Virtual Vault and First Virtual, not to mention trying to figure out how Microsoft, Netscape, IBM, and all the other big computer companies fit into the picture.

This book will attempt to make some sense out of the confusion that seems to reign in the world of electronic commerce, particularly when it comes to identifying software companies that are providing solutions in the market. Electronic commerce itself is too huge a field to be conquered in one book, considering that digital trade encompasses not only transactions conducted over the Internet, but also over electronic data interchange (EDI), wire transfer, and other electronic formats. Even Internet commerce is a broad business that includes not only Web-based transactions but all trade that occurs on corporate intranets, extranets, and over other Internet facilities such as e-mail and file transfer protocol (FTP). Therefore, to try to keep the focus within a manageable scope and provide some useful material that will help executives make decisions about what solutions might be best for them, this book will look at the business of Web commerce, defined as the practice of selling goods and services over the World Wide Web.

We will address issues faced by both small and large companies, and present solutions for both business-to-consumer and business-to-business models. The purpose of this book is to help businesspeople, from business unit managers up to CEOs, try to answer some of the following questions:

➤ What are my goals for setting up a Web commerce system?
➤ Where do I start?
➤ Who are the major players?
➤ How much will it cost?
➤ How do I build it?
➤ How much time will it take?
➤ Can I make any money?
➤ What are other companies doing?

To address these issues, *Web Commerce* is organized into four parts. Part I, "The Web: A New Business Model," includes an overview of the Web commerce marketplace, projections for growth, strategies for formulating a Web commerce business plan, and two case studies that highlight the very different approaches taken by a small and a large business that have set up shop on the Web. Part II, "Putting the Pieces Together," looks at some of the major commerce solutions from entry-level electronic storefront software through high-end transactional systems, payment options, and security solutions. Part III, "Industry Applications," provides in-depth information about successful Web commerce businesses across a range of industries. Part IV, "Cashing In on Web Commerce," discusses impacts of Web commerce to the organization as well as to the distribution channel, which for business-to-business commerce is probably the biggest issue for companies exploring this new model.

This book is not meant to be a complete guide to all of the electronic commerce solution providers. There are too many to cover. Rather, it will present options for both small and large companies looking at implementing online businesses, focusing on some of the major software solutions and third-party providers. There is no single model for Web commerce, or one way of implementing a solution, regardless of the size and complexity of your business.

To demonstrate how disparate the solutions and pricing can be for a single Web site, consider this: In September 1996, *Advertising Age*'s "Net Marketing" supplement conducted a survey of Web site developers to come up with a national Web Price Index for site development. It issued an RFP to Web site developers across the country for the creation of Web sites for three businesses—small, medium, and large—each with specific requirements. What came back was a price differential of almost 2,000 percent! For a large Web site with secure transactional capabilities integrated with back-end systems, site design with dynamic page generation, as well as site promotion, the median price was $596,000. However, one developer proposed creating the site for just $15,000, while another wanted $2.8 million. This shows just how difficult it can be to try to recommend specific solutions for electronic commerce.

This book will present a range of options for setting up commerce-enabled Web sites. It will provide in-depth information on more than two dozen electronic commerce product and service providers, including pricing, features, benefits, implementation requirements, and the target market for these solutions.

Perhaps of even greater value, this book will provide in-the-trenches information from more than a dozen companies that are now conducting commerce from their Web sites. These case studies will look at each company's goals, the approach it took to evaluating and selecting commerce solutions, how the systems are set up, how they work, and how they're solving critical business problems. Also, it will look at some of the things that went wrong during the projects, and pitfalls to avoid in the future.

Moreover, this book will provide analysis on which models work and which don't, what steps businesses need to take to implement their own Web commerce plans, and advice from analysts and early adopters of Web commerce.

So read it and take from it what you need. There are plenty of checklists, charts, and summaries to help you formulate your Web commerce plans and start implementing solutions. If you're a small business looking at setting up an electronic storefront, you may not need to know about $250,000 end-to-end solutions from third-party providers like Open Market or about building a $10 million site in-house like NECX. But you'll probably find some useful strategies and interesting war stories that could apply to your business.

If you're spending millions on IS resources to design and build a system from scratch, you might be interested in learning about third-party software packages that weren't available two to three years ago but may work for you now.

Remember, *there's no one way to do this*. Web commerce is still in its infancy. The companies that have started down this route are still learning lessons and figuring out what makes sense for them. The important thing is to get started now, before all your competitors figure it out.

Part I
The Web: A New Business Model

Chapter **1**

Web Commerce Grows Up

On the hype-reality meter, electronic commerce is finally starting to register on the reality side. It has taken more than four years, since the first companies started putting up sites on the World Wide Web in 1994. Back then, the Web was more about show biz—about broadcasting live Rolling Stones concerts over the Internet and hooking up Nintendo players around the world—rather than a place to conduct serious business.

Randall Whiting, president and CEO of electronic commerce research consortium CommerceNet, recalls his experience in 1993 of trying to convince senior executives at Hewlett-Packard (HP), one of the trade group's highest-profile members, of the need to put up a Web site, to which they responded, "Why would we want a Web site? We're not Walt Disney. We're not a gaming company. Why would serious HP want a Web site?"

Why would serious HP want a Web site indeed? Why would any company doing business anywhere in the world want a Web site? To sell products and services. To reach new customers and create new ways of transacting business with suppliers, trading partners, investors, and other constituents. To make money.

HP quickly saw the light and launched a Web site in 1994, along with about 600 other companies. Today, there are more than 8 million commercial (.com) Web sites.

As corporations are now discovering, the Web is having a profound impact on how they conduct business. With its open-platform-based technology and ubiquitous reach, the Internet is allowing companies to open up new distribution channels, forge communities of buyers and sellers, increase revenues, and boost the bottom line. In ways unimaginable just four years ago, corporations are utilizing Internet technology to set up electronic commerce businesses and successfully conduct trade over the Internet. Here are just a few examples:

➤ Cisco Connection Online, a business-to-business commerce site, is now selling $11 million in networking equipment a day, at an annual rate of $4 billion — roughly 60 percent of Cisco Systems' total revenue.

➤ Dell Computers is selling $5 million a day, at an annual rate of $1.8 billion, from its Web site.

➤ Microsoft's Expedia travel service sells $4 million a week, or more than $200 million a year, in airline tickets from its site.

➤ NECX's online computer store sells $5 million worth of computer-related products each month over its Web site, about $60 million a year.

➤ Ticketmaster sold $35 million in tickets on its Web site in 1997, roughly 3 percent of its total ticket sales; in 1998, it expects to sell about $90 million in tickets on its site.

➤ 1-800-FLOWERS generates $30 million a year, roughly 10 percent of its total sales, on the Internet.

■ WEB COMMERCE GROWTH

The growth in Web commerce might be likened to a hockey stick curve, starting out fairly flat for the first year or so of its development, then skyrocketing. Consider these markers:

➤ In January 1995, consumers polled by the Gallup Organization and CMP Media's *Interactive Age* magazine said purchasing products was the single *least* compelling reason for going online, outranked by gathering news and information, communicating with friends and colleagues, doing database searches, accessing games and software, participating in chats and forums, and conducting electronic polling, voting, or town meetings, in that order.

➤ By the fall of 1995, according to a survey by CommerceNet and Nielsen Media Research, 55 percent of Web users said they went online to look for specific product information, while 35 percent of Web users looked for product information before making an actual purchase, although not necessarily in cyberspace. In fact, at the time the survey was done, very few Web sites were conducting electronic commerce.

➤ In its "1996 Online Project" report, Jupiter Communications projected that Web-based shopping revenues would jump from $407.3 million in 1996 to $1.1 billion in 1997, reaching $4.5 billion in 2000.

➤ In an October 1996 report, Forrester Research Inc. projected that the total U.S. Internet economy would approach $200 billion by 2000, which includes infrastructure, Internet access, consumer commerce, and business-to-business commerce. According to the report, by 2000 business-to-business e-commerce trade and fees would reach $66 billion, consumer online retail transactions and fees would reach $7.1 billion, and the sale of content over the Net would grow to $4.8 billion.

➤ In March 1997, in a follow-up to the CommerceNet/ Nielsen survey, 73 percent of Web users said they spent time online looking for specific product information, while 53 percent looked for product information online before making a purchase. And 15 percent—roughly 5.6 million people—made actual purchases online.

➤ In March 1997, the Yankee Group estimated that sales of consumer goods over the Internet would total $2.7 billion in 1997, reaching $10 billion by 2000. Sales of business-to-business goods over the Internet were expected to be $540 million in 1997, reaching $134 billion by 2000.

➤ In July 1997, Computer Economics said the total value of purchases over the Internet would grow from $40 billion in 1998 to close to $120 billion by 2000, with the average annual expenditure per purchaser at just over $2,500 by 2000.

➤ In November 1997, Forrester issued a report with updated revenue projections for electronic commerce: By 2001, online retail revenues would reach $17 billion, while business-to-business electronic commerce would generate $183 billion.

➤ In April 1998, ActivMedia issued a report that predicted electronic commerce revenues would total $1.2 *trillion* by 2002.

■ FACTORS DRIVING GROWTH

Here are some of the key reasons why Web commerce is taking off:

➤ There are now more than 60 million Internet users, and more than 50 million Web users, according to International Data Corp.

➤ One-third of the 1.1 million U.S. businesses will be connected to the Internet by 2000, according to Forrester.

➤ More than 20 million users have made purchases online, and that number will grow to more than 40 million by 2000, according to Computer Economics.

■ WHICH INDUSTRIES WILL THRIVE?

What are people buying online? The No. 1 purchase item is computer hardware and software, according to several research groups, including Yankee, Forrester, Jupiter, and CommerceNet. According to Forrester, sales of computer products will generate nearly one-third—or $2.1 billion—of total online shopping revenues of $6.6 billion. The No. 2 online purchase item, according to Forrester, is travel, followed by entertainment, apparel, gifts and flowers, food and drink, and other products.

New York research firm Jupiter Communications Inc. is even hotter on travel. It predicts that by 2000, travel will account for $3 billion of a total $6 billion in Web transaction revenues. Based on findings from the CommerceNet/Nielsen survey, the No. 2 purchase item for those actually buying online now is printed materials such as magazines, books, and newsletters, while for those just looking for product information online before making a purchase, the No. 2 category is information related to automotive purchases.

While everyone has a different take on which industries are best positioned to capitalize on electronic commerce (e-commerce), it's becoming increasingly clear that just about every business must be looking at whether it should be implementing an e-commerce strategy.

In its January 1997 report "ECS Scenarios," the Gartner Group projects that by 2000, 60 percent of worldwide enterprises will be engaged in some form of electronic commerce. Says Gartner analyst Barbara Reilly, "By 1998, the largest obstacles to commercial development of the Internet will have been resolved, and the pressure for every business to get on the Net will be irresistible."

■ WHICH WEB COMMERCE MODELS WILL WORK?

There are lots of ways at looking at Web commerce, and depending on what kind of business you're in, you'll want to develop a plan that works best for your unique operations, whether you're selling candy or routers.

"What's interesting about electronic commerce is, it's not such a new idea," says Brian Kirk, senior manager of information, communications, and entertainment (ICE) at consulting firm KPMG Peat Marwick LLP. "The Web has given it a sexy currency." Kirk believes the real benefits that Internet-based technologies will provide in the near term are linking trading partners in a supply chain and automating business processes to make their transactions more efficient, including delivery services such as Federal Express offering electronic tracking services to business customers, and retailers such as Wal-Mart hooking up over private or public networks to the inventory and ordering systems of suppliers.

Other analysts, consultants, and business professionals agree that the real benefits of Web-based and more broadly defined electronic commerce-based technologies will be to the business-to-business sector, as demonstrated by companies such as Cisco Systems Inc. which are now making billions in this niche by selling directly to other businesses over the Internet. In fact, those companies now conducting business-to-business commerce argue that misinterpretations about electronic commerce and Web commerce will hurt the industry in the short term.

"So many people focus on commerce from a consumer perspective, which I think is crap," said Chris Sinton, senior manager of Cisco Connection Online in mid-1997.

"Consumer commerce has been a red herring. With all there is in the media about ordering books, wine, and flowers over the Internet, businesses are sitting out there not figuring out ways to really utilize the technology." Cisco, a networking equipment manufacturer, obviously has a stake in the business as it tries to sell its products to big companies that are spending tremendous amounts of money to create huge systems linking buyers, sellers, and other third parties through complex networks. But the truth is, consumer commerce sites such as online bookstore Amazon.com, wine merchant Virtual Vineyards, 1-800-FLOWERS, and hundreds of other online merchants, are doing fantastic business on the Web, and their models are certainly valid. And for businesses that don't have millions to spend and want to reach larger audiences, there are many low-cost ways of setting up online shops, through third-party providers or low-cost catalog software.

Case in point: Caribbean tour operator Horizon Tours in Washington, DC, wanted to put its business online but didn't have a lot of money to spend. What it ended up doing was not at all what it set out to do, as will be discussed in Chapter 2, and the company is still not making significant money on the Web. However, it is only spending about $700 a month to experiment with online commerce, and it broke even after two years. The important thing learned by Horizon is that the Web represents a way to expand business and create entirely new selling models.

However, business executives that have pursued a certain model are sure that theirs, and few like it, are the only ones worth merit. "There will be very few models that work," emphatically states Henry Bertolon, president and CEO of NECX, an independent distributor of semiconductors and computer products whose NECX Web site is selling $5 million a month online. He says there's room for consumer and business-to-business commerce, but only for certain models:

➤ Niche products with high margins and low volume.
➤ Niche products with low margins and high volume.

For the first model, Bertolon gives the example of hand-knitted Afghan sweaters being sold over the Web, and for the second model, he uses his own business as an example: selling semi-conductors, computers, and networking equipment in a vertical value-added network to manufacturers and corporate Information Technology (IT) buyers.

■ REFERENCES

ActivMedia, "The Real Numbers Behind Net Profits 1997," 1997.

ActivMedia, "The Real Numbers Behind Net Profits 1998," 1998.

Alliance for Converging Technologies, "The Future of Electronic Commerce: Profiting in the Web Marketspace," 1996.

Forrester Research, "Sizing the Internet Economy: Money," Sept./Oct. 1996.

The Gallup Organization/CMP Publications Inc., "Consumer Study," Interactive Age, Jan. 30, 1995, p. 46.

Gartner Group, "Electronic Commerce Services Scenarios," Jan. 1997.

Jupiter Communications, "1996 Online Project," Jan. 1997.

Nielsen Media Research/CommerceNet, "Internet Demographics Survey," Oct. 1995.

Nielsen Media Research/CommerceNet, "Internet Demographic and Electronic Commerce Study," Mar. 1997.

Chapter 2

A New Horizon: One Small Business' Web Commerce Story

Eddie Lloyd represents a breed of entrepreneurs that want to take advantage of Internet technology to grow their businesses, and his story symbolizes both the frustrations and the opportunities that can arise when mom-and-pop (or in this case, mom-and-son) businesses try to jump on the Internet bandwagon without really knowing what they're getting into.

Lloyd is regional sales director of Horizon Tours, a Washington, DC–based travel firm owned by his mother, Dimple Morrow, that packages Caribbean vacations primarily for travel agencies, although it does some retail travel as a small percentage of its business. In business since 1983 and generating annual revenues of about $3 million, Horizon has experienced the roller-coaster ride that travel firms have been through in recent years as a result of cost cutting from the big airlines and competition coming in from new, bare-bones carriers.

Horizon's commerce story began in 1995, when major airline companies began to implement commission caps paid to travel agents for booking flights. Prior to the caps, travel agents could expect to earn about 10 percent in commission on reservations, which amounted to some pretty nice money when booking international flights at $5,000 a ticket. But with the caps implemented by the airlines, travel agencies were looking at a $50 maximum commission for booking flights, forcing them to radically rethink ways of doing business.

"With the caps, we came to realize that the travel industry was changing, and if you didn't ride with the change, and change with the change, you were going to be crushed," said Lloyd. About this time, the Internet was just starting to get hot, so Horizon started to look at the new technology as a way to expand its business and get more competitive.

"We've always been technology conscious," said Lloyd, pointing out that for years Horizon had been communicating with its clients electronically, first with faxes and more recently with e-mail over an account it maintained with USNet, a Maryland-based Internet access provider. So Horizon thought putting up a Web site would be a great way to achieve the following goals:

1. To demonstrate to its clients that it is a forward-thinking and responsive company.
2. To better communicate with travel agencies and other clients.
3. To expand its business by reaching new users.

■ FROM WEB ILLITERATE TO WEBMASTER

Horizon was in the same boat as a lot of other businesses that wanted to test the Internet waters when the Web was first gaining a foothold in 1994 and 1995. "We didn't even know what HTML meant," said Lloyd, referring to the hypertext markup language that's used to convert electronic documents to Web format. So in late 1995, Horizon hired a Web developer to build its site, relying on the very first consultant who happened to knock on its door offering services. When asked what he found impressive about this consultant, Lloyd was honest. "He didn't impress us at all," he said. In fact, the Web developer, who was Russian, barely spoke English. But he had a portfolio and offered to do the whole site for $200, so Horizon hired him. Hosting the site at USNet for $29 a month, "it was dirt cheap," said Lloyd. But he quickly realized he was getting what he paid for: not much. The site was basically a Caribbean brochure on the Web, with no interactive capabilities or new ways of reaching users.

There were other problems as well. Basically it boiled down to relinquishing control of the site to someone else. Every time content had to be changed or added, Horizon would pass it along to the Web developer, who would incorporate the changes in a dummy format, and then Horizon would proof them before they could be implemented. It was a tedious process.

Then, in April 1996, AT&T announced Easy World Wide Web (EW3), a Web site developing and hosting service for businesses priced at $295 a month for existing AT&T customers and $395 a month for non-AT&T customers. At the time it was first released, EW3 included secure Web hosting, registration of a unique domain name, Microsoft FrontPage Web authoring software, a two-day training session, and other support services.

Horizon found out about EW3 through its AT&T long-distance account manager and was immediately interested in the service because of the reliability it associated with AT&T. Lloyd said that would translate into quality for clients. Not only that, but AT&T's approach in working with its clients appealed to Horizon.

"The first thing that attracted us to AT&T was their focus on helping small businesses grow," said Dimple Morrow, who is Jamaican. "They were offering training that would enable us to create and develop our own Web site. Before, the control of the site was in someone else's hands. Now, we could really put our heart and soul into something that was very dear to us." By this time, Horizon was ready to gamble a little more money on its Web site, hoping the payoff would be there if it could attract more business. So it became a beta test site for EW3 and Lloyd took off for a two-day training class in Lincroft, New Jersey, to learn how to design a Web site. "When I came back, I was on the Net. I was surfing. I was out there," said Lloyd. He knew how to do HTML. He was cool. So he took the shell of what had been the Horizon Web site, which was basically a map of Jamaica with links to various parts of the island, and developed a more complete, graphically enriched site with FrontPage, a Web development tool that Microsoft acquired from Vermeer Technologies. On the new site was a more current listing of what to see and do in Jamaica, with links to outside references, and more pictures and more color developed with FrontPage. With the training he'd received, Lloyd was able to create a better structure for the site with more sophisticated navigation.

One of the images Horizon decided to add to its site was a map of the District of Columbia showing Horizon's main offices, "Three blocks from Bill (Clinton)'s house." Here's why: "One of the problems with online entities is credibility," said Lloyd. "Anybody can throw up a shingle and become a Web business. The map is on the site so people can see where Horizon Tours is. If we were fraudulent, we probably wouldn't want to set up shop three blocks from the White House." From the time Lloyd started developing the site, it took about one month to get it up and running.

But then came the next challenge. Said Lloyd, "Nobody knew our site was there. I had the buckets ready to catch the money. We just knew it would keep pouring in, but the buckets just sat there."

He remembers what it was like those first few days, sitting around waiting for the hits to come in. The first visits were from AT&T trainers who had coached Lloyd in developing his site. Then came visits from friends and family. Finally, business started trickling in, but not until Horizon

learned how to promote the site through links on search engine sites like Yahoo! and Lycos, and on other travel-related
sites. And the process of submitting forms for online links
became a job in itself, one that Lloyd spent hours a week on.

"Part of our long-term focus was whenever we found related sites, we'd offer them an exchange," said Lloyd. "We'll
provide a link to your site if you provide a link to ours." This
approach worked well for Horizon, and through it the site
got visibility on high-traffic sites such as the Travel Channel
(www.travelchannel.com), Holiday Beach Hotel & Casino in
Curaçao (hol-beach.com), and the Orlando Mall (theorlan-
domall.com). By October 1996, Horizon's traffic was up to
1,000 hits per week, resulting in increased exposure, which
drove more business to Horizon. But Horizon still hadn't realized the potential it had hoped for on the Internet. It
wanted to see some return on its investment, small though it
was, and it knew it needed to find a way to use the Web to
conduct real business.

■ READY FOR COMMERCE

When AT&T started talking about offering commerce services as part of its Web site family of products, Horizon was
ready. "AT&T found in us a guinea pig," said Lloyd. That's because Horizon was eager to try new things and didn't mind
taking risks. "When they said, 'We have commerce going on,'
we said, 'Let's jump on that.'"

So Horizon became another beta test site for SecureBuy,
which AT&T officially announced in October 1996 as a "cyber-
soup-to-nuts solution" for secure buying and selling on the Internet. The SecureBuy service is integrated with transactional
software from Open Market Inc. and includes credit card authorization and processing, order tracking, management reports, and other features (see Chapter 4).

SecureBuy costs $395 a month in addition to the host-
ing fees, so Horizon was now spending about $700 a month

for its commerce site. But Lloyd was convinced he'd soon be making money and was ready to step up his investment.

He headed to Lincroft for another training session. By this time, did he feel like a Web expert? "No, I felt like a retard," he said. "Doing commerce is a whole new thing."

The biggest difference between information and commerce on a site is that when people are actually spending money, you can't afford to be wrong. Therefore, in calculating total product costs, including shipping and taxes, companies have to be careful to be exact. "Short of having some sort of online database set up, we just did not see that there was a simple way of making it happen," said Lloyd, pointing to the complexity of packaging online tours, which includes volatile rates for air travel, hotels, transportation, local attractions, and other frequently changing information. "We realized it would be totally difficult to put a price on the Internet that is fixed," said Lloyd. "We didn't want to have a Web site with tons and tons of choices." While trying to figure out how to commerce-enable its site, Horizon started the process of working with its existing banks to set up an Internet storefront, and this turned out to be the biggest challenge of all, said Lloyd. In its physical business, Horizon works with several banks, including Citibank, NationsBank, and First Union, to process credit cards, checks, and other transactions. In order to process credit card transactions over the Net, companies must first have an Internet merchant ID account, and while Horizon had merchant ID accounts with its existing banks, it needed a separate merchant ID account for Internet commerce.

Because there's a high degree of credit card fraud in the travel industry, banks are often reluctant to set up Internet merchant accounts for travel agencies, and Horizon kept getting turned down. Eventually, it figured out it would have to sell something else.

"When you go to the Caribbean, you want to bring part of your experience back with you," said Lloyd. Jamaica is known for its coffee, spices, arts, and crafts. So Horizon decided to sell Jamaican coffee from its site, teaming up with Atlanta coffee importer J. Martinez & Co. He got an Internet merchant ID card from Credit Card Services International, and was ready to start selling coffee on his site.

Timing is everything. Lloyd was scheduled to speak at an AT&T user workshop in early 1997, and he wanted to demonstrate his Web commerce site. So he called his AT&T support representative at 4 P.M. the afternoon before the conference and said, "I want to be able to sell coffee by tomorrow." No problem. Lloyd had all the information on paper, and with guidance from the support representative on the phone, he input it into FrontPage using a wizard that set up his store. All he needed to do was key in data such as product number, product ID, description, and other attributes. After he entered his store information, AT&T tested the site. If something wasn't working, it was fixed while Lloyd waited. By the end of the phone call, two-and-a-half hours later, his site was up and running. (See Figure 2.1.)

■ EXPANDING HORIZON'S ONLINE BUSINESS

Selling coffee turned out to be a fairly successful business for Horizon. By the spring of 1997, the site was generating more than $500 a month, and Lloyd was encouraged enough to add new products to his Web site. He was still losing money, but he thought that if he could find the right mix of travel-related products, he could turn a profit by the end of the year. So he started selling a Jamaican travel book, a Jamaican music CD, and Jamaican spices. In February 1998, he started selling AT&T digital phones, for which he earns about $50 apiece, at an average rate of 25 units per month. "Why should we stop at travel?" ponders Lloyd. "We're selling coffee, and we don't know jack about coffee. This has almost created a business in and of itself."

Lloyd was turning into a real Web development pro, too. Using tools provided by AT&T and downloading software

Figure 2.1. Horizon Tours sells Caribbean tours, coffee, music, books, and other products from its Web store.

from the Web, Lloyd was integrating multimedia capabilities into his site. For example, to promote the CD, Horizon used TrueSpeech digital sound compression technology that he downloaded to his IBM Aptiva PC from DSG Group's Web site at www.dsgp.com. When he first attempted to do this, AT&T's server did not support TrueSpeech software. But at Lloyd's request, AT&T added some lines of code to its setup service to accommodate the sound program. After building the application with FrontPage on his PC, he uploaded it to AT&T's server. Eventually, Lloyd got so good at building Web applications that he started developing sites for Jamaican hotels featured on his site. "It's gotten to the point where my mom is ready to fire me so I can work only on the Internet," says Lloyd.

The site began turning a profit in mid-1998. And while Horizon is now selling enough to support its Web operations, the real benefit is the site's power as a lead generator, says Lloyd.

■ SMALL-BUSINESS LESSONS

Many lessons can be learned from Horizon's experience in Web commerce. On the downside, Horizon made the following mistakes:

1. It trusted the first so-called Web expert who came calling. Fortunately, its investment wasn't that large.
2. It assumed that its existing methods of conducting financial transactions—namely, with its banks—could be easily transferred to the Internet.
3. It thought that once the site was up, people would find it.
4. It didn't really think through what it was trying to do before launching its Web business: specifically, that travel is a complicated business and might not transfer easily to Web commerce.

On the positive side, Horizon succeeded by doing the following things:

1. It recognized the opportunity of the Internet at an early stage and started exploring options.
2. It wasn't afraid to fail.
3. It realized that in order to be competitive, it would need to rethink existing ways of doing business.
4. It was aggressive in learning the technology and implementing applications.
5. It quickly rebounded from failed efforts to set up an online travel business and created an alternative Web commerce business selling coffee, spices, music, and other products.

6. It found ways to cross-promote the site through other travel-related sites.

Here's what Lloyd has to say about his experience in Web commerce:

Too many people have more money than you do to throw at something. The Internet is a great equalizer. It makes me as big as the next guy. In the end, you'll still be bigger than me, but we can be the best by being very, very good at what we do.

And this is what he says it takes to be the best at Web commerce:

1. Put a lot of time into your Web site.
2. Be creative.
3. Give people a reason to keep coming back, such as giveaways and free information.
4. Sell quality products.
5. Provide a way for people to give you feedback about what you're doing.

Horizon is a good example of a small business that's beginning to figure out the Web commerce business without spending a ton of money to do so. In the next chapter, we'll look at the other extreme: a very large business, Cisco Systems, which is spending millions of dollars on a business-to-business Web commerce site to sell products to customers. And its payoff? Billions.

Cisco's $4 Billion Web Site

You can't go from $2 billion to $4 billion in one year without doing business a whole new way.

Chris Sinton
senior manager, Cisco Connection Online

Cisco Systems Inc. is one of the best examples to date of a successful Web commerce business. Cisco, a San Jose, California, company that makes internet working gear like routers, hubs, and switches, saw its business double from $2 billion in 1995 to $4 billion in 1996 as companies around the world invested heavily in networking-related products. Fueled largely by the boom of the Internet, the phenomenal growth presented both a danger and an opportunity for Cisco. The danger: Not being able to support the increased business, particularly with regard to sales support and customer service. The opportunity: Demonstrating by example the power of the Internet to solve critical business problems and, therefore, driving even more networking business.

"We needed to find new and better ways to scale the organization," said Chris Sinton, senior manager of Cisco Connection Online (CCO), Cisco's business-to-business commerce Web site at www.cisco.com. For example, in 1995, Cisco received 350,000 faxed orders from its direct business customers and resale partners, all of which had to be keyed into the computer system, sucking up the valuable time of customer service representatives that could have been better spent servicing customers and developing relationships. "We didn't think we could scale to 700,000 (faxed orders)," remarked Sinton. "Our unprecedented growth forced us to develop new means of conducting business faster, cheaper, and more efficiently."

That new means is CCO, Cisco's "networked commerce" site on the Web that lets its business customers and direct resale partners order from more than 12,000 Cisco products online, as well as access service and support functions such as product pricing, product configuration, and order status. Since its launch in July 1996, CCO has achieved the following milestones:

➤ Generates $11 million a day, or $4 billion a year.

➤ Processes 1,000 online orders per day.

➤ Achieves $360 million in cost savings a year.

➤ Generates 60 percent of Cisco's total revenues over the Web.

➤ Has registered 34,000 customer sites that order Cisco products exclusively online.

While these numbers are impressive and have gotten Cisco good press, an interesting part of the story is that Cisco says it never set out to make any additional revenue from the site. "Money is not the driving factor," said Sinton, who helped create the vision for CCO in 1995 when he was manger of literature distribution services in Cisco's marketing department. He now runs CCO from a smallish office crammed with Asian art, techno toys, and strategy-laden marker boards.

Cisco Connection Online is a good example of how a business is using the Web to automate daily operations, make its employees more efficient, and improve relationships with customers and partners. And while creating additional revenue wasn't an explicit goal of CCO from the start, the site is bringing in incremental money (such as $10 million alone through the sale of Cisco mugs and T-shirts online), and the resulting efficiencies are boosting Cisco's bottom line.

How much, the company won't or can't say, but Cisco is definitely seeing a significant return on the $3 million or so it initially put into the site.

CCO helps to illustrate the dilemma facing business-to-business companies as they evaluate launching Web commerce ventures: Business-to-business commerce is expected to make up the bulk of electronic commerce revenues by the year 2000. International Data Corp., a Framingham, Massachusetts, research firm, reports that of the $116 billion expected to be generated in Internet sales by the new millennium, 70 percent will come from business-to-business transactions.

At the same time, business-to-business companies are concerned that launching Web commerce sites could disrupt their existing sales channels. For example, at Cisco, 70 percent of total revenue is generated through resale partners such as AT&T, Siemens, and Alcatel, and these resellers have turf to protect. Launching a Web commerce operation threatens to cut them out of the loop, and Cisco doesn't want to burn them, thereby hurting its own business. So what to do?

This chapter will look at:

➤ Cisco's networked commerce strategy.

➤ How it built its Web commerce system.

➤ How much it cost.

➤ How it works.

Further, this chapter will examine:

➤ How Cisco's customers and trading partners are benefiting from the system.

➤ How Cisco overcame initial resistance from customers and its own employees.

➤ What makes the online operation successful.

➤ Advice to other businesses that want to set up Web commerce shops.

■ CISCO'S NETWORKED COMMERCE STRATEGY

As a high-tech company specializing in networking products, Cisco was naturally an early adopter in the Internet arena. The company started providing electronic software downloads over FTP and technical support over e-mail and to its customers in 1985. In 1994, it launched Cisco Information Online, a public Web site that offered company and product information as well as technical support.

In mid-1996, when Cisco was coping with its phenomenal growth, it embarked on a new Internet strategy. "We changed our objectives to look at the network as a means to turn the company inside out, provide access to commerce, expand service and support, and truly enable many different organizations within the company," said Sinton.

It calls this strategy *Networked Commerce,* which in the broadest sense means leveraging the enterprise network to foster interactive relationships with prospects, customers, partners, suppliers, and employees. With CCO, Cisco is providing an end-to-end solution for automating sales transactions. But the strategy, which now permeates the entire organization, was spawned from the marketing department in 1995.

Sinton said that when he was in charge of distributing marketing materials, he began to poke around the Web and thought, "This is a cool thing. I can sell these marketing products online." His concept was to transfer the paper, fax, e-mail, and CD-ROM distribution of marketing support material such as technical documentation and training materials to the Web, thereby saving time for Cisco's employees, customers, and trading partners, freeing them up to concentrate on more substantial tasks.

He presented his idea in a Cisco sector meeting, which is company jargon for a meeting with more than one vice president in the room. Attending this particular meeting were president and CEO John Chambers, as well as marketing and IS executives. Sinton went through his spiel, trying to make the executives aware of what could be done with the technology, after which Chambers turned to the marketing and IS executives and said, "You guys should talk about this and better understand how to do it," according to Sinton.

So more meetings ensued, during which Sinton and his colleagues put together a plan for the commerce idea. Among the concepts discussed were:

1. Who should manage the site.
2. How the applications should be developed.
3. How the infrastructure should be built.

At the base of the structure was IS Operations, an IS organization that would develop the main infrastructure for the site. On top of IS Operations was interactive technologies, another IS organization that would develop the key technologies necessary to support the commerce applications, such as automating the electronic distribution of documentation. Finally, and central to the proposal, was a group called *interactive marketing tools,* a centralized group whose goal would be to ensure a consistent and cohesive site. IMT would work with all the departments, such as human resources, marketing, finance, customer service, and others, to get their input. "What's important is that the whole company would be developing Web applications," said Sinton.

However, despite the initial enthusiasm expressed by Sinton and members of the group working on the proposal, the implementation turned out to be tougher than expected. "Marketing had this wild-ass idea that we could do this, but I was a little naive," he admits. His naiveté came from thinking it would be a relatively easy matter to create a commerce site capable of providing the transactional capabilities he had in mind. At the time, there were virtually no turnkey solutions or Web site developers with a track record developing complex commerce sites. Sinton got a couple of proposals from local developers, but he quickly realized his expectations were greater than what the providers could deliver. "We got the proposals back, and the scope was beyond what the agencies could deal with," he said. "It was hard to get anyone to understand it."

The biggest challenge facing the developers of Cisco's commerce site was multiple legacy systems that needed to be integrated into the Web commerce application, namely pricing, product configuration, and order management systems that were based on Oracle databases running on big Sun servers. "We realized we needed to get help from IS," Sinton explained.

➤ IS to the Rescue

After it realized that third-party providers would not be capable of providing complete solutions for Cisco's Web commerce site, Sinton and his staff turned to the IS department to build the site. Like other companies starting down the road to electronic commerce, Cisco began by gathering people from marketing, IS, and customer support to define the objectives and create a roadmap for the system.

While the initial idea for the commerce part of the site was to sell marketing and marketing support materials online, it soon became apparent that the real benefit of the site would be to automate many of the functions within customer support or what Cisco calls *customer advocacy.*

Customer advocacy is the largest division of Cisco and garners significant support within the organization. Everything the company does revolves around servicing Cisco's customers, and this philosophy is apparent from the way the business has been organized to prop up customer advocacy. For example, unlike many other large businesses that place

IS in a separate line reporting to the CEO, Cisco's CIO, Pete Solvik, reports to Doug Allred, the executive vice president of customer advocacy.

"It (dedication to customer support) totally puts us at the forefront of what we do," says Susan Aragon, IS manager of networked commerce for Cisco customer advocacy, who led the development of the commerce applications for CCO. "I build solutions for Cisco customers, whereas most traditional IS groups build solutions for the enterprise."

Aragon said that from the very beginning of the project, much of the development of the commerce site was driven by the customer advocacy group. To develop the strategy and applications for the site, Cisco assembled two teams: A business side team and an IS team. This is the usual way of starting a Web commerce project or any other type of system implementation at a major corporation.

On the business team were four product managers and two customer support people for the first commerce applications that would be developed for the site, which included the following modules:

➤ Pricing.
➤ Ordering.
➤ Configuration.
➤ Order status.

On the IS side were four dedicated developers and two ancillary staffers. Working together at Cisco's Santa Clara facility, which houses customer support, the two groups interacted frequently to figure out which applications to develop first and how to build them.

Also central to the project, Cisco created a Networked Commerce Advisory Board (NCAB) made up of 40-plus direct customers and resale partners who provided input for the site. "The best way to be successful is to understand exactly what your customers want," said Todd Elizalde, senior manager of networked commerce for Cisco customer advocacy.

However, Cisco later found out that it should have gotten NCAB involved even earlier and more deeply; this is discussed later in this chapter.

Writing the applications mainly with C programming language, CGI (common gateway interface) scripts, and HTML, the IS staff developed practically the entire site in-house. "We didn't use anything fancy," said Aragon, pointing out that there were no Java applets or ActiveX development tools available at the time. She said that had there been these types of tools, as well as turnkey solutions for transaction processing, Cisco probably would have used them. "We want to use third-party applications where it makes sense," she said. "We don't particularly want to be in the software application development business."

Cisco did use a few tools where it made sense. For example, when building the configuration component, with which users configure products based on their system requirements and specifications, Cisco used the CAIT rules-based engine from Calico Technologies. Configuring network products is a very complicated business, particularly because virtually every component in the network is dependent to some extent upon other network components. When ordering a product such as a Cisco 7513 router, for example, customers need to let the ordering system know how each slot in the router is to be configured. While it could have written this code alone, the IS team found a really useful tool in the CAIT engine, which pulls information from Cisco's manufacturer bills of materials, running on an Oracle database behind the corporate firewall, to make sure that every possible network contingency is accounted for. The system is virtually foolproof when it comes to preventing mistakes made when ordering, which has turned into a very big benefit for Cisco and its customers. One other third-party piece of software Cisco used was a security package from Talarian, which secures the transaction between the server and Cisco's firewall.

The development of the commerce part of CCO, which is primarily located in the Internetworking Product Center of the site, took roughly 10 months, from September 1995 to July

1996, although some of the components were introduced to beta customers and rolled out in phases. The cost of the site was roughly $3 million, the bulk of which was salaries. In addition, Cisco purchased two Sun Enterprise 5000 servers priced at roughly $40,000 apiece, as well as Netscape Commerce Server software and the third-party packages.

When the site was completed, it contained the following commerce applications:

➤ *Configuration agent:* Permits users to configure Cisco's complex networking products.

➤ *Pricing agent:* Permits Cisco resellers and customers to price out products, including discounts based on their status.

➤ *Order status agent:* Provides direct customers and resellers with a status of orders, including a complete backlog of company orders and proof of delivery. In addition, users can link to the Web sites of Federal Express, HPS, and DHL to get detailed delivery information on their order. This is the most popular feature of the site.

➤ *Invoice agent:* Allows direct customers and resellers to access their invoices online.

➤ *Service order:* Allows Cisco customers and resellers to check the status on service orders placed or conducted.

➤ *Contract status:* Enables customers to check the status of their contracts.

➤ *Lead time agent:* Permits resellers to check the lead times on Cisco products.

The Internetworking Product Center, which is the heart of the commerce part of CCO, is available to three audiences: the general public, Cisco direct customers, and resale partners. Before they can use certain elements of CCO, such as the pricing agent, customers must have a Cisco maintenance contract, priced starting at about $100, and they must register for the site, providing information to identify themselves and their companies. In addition to

standard ID information, direct customers must also provide an example of a past Cisco order, and specify which
company users are authorized to make buying decisions.
These steps are taken to protect not only Cisco's proprietary
data, but customer and resale partner data as well. Finally,
customers and resale partners must sign a paper contract
stating that in the future, all ordering will be done over CCO.

Nonregistered guests have access to the following
applications:

➤ Cisco product information.

➤ Cisco job listings.

➤ Listings of Cisco seminars and events.

➤ Other company information.

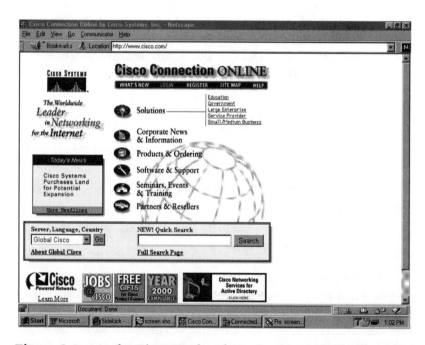

Figure 3.1. At the Cisco Marketplace, users can configure, price,
and order internet working products, as well as Cisco promotional
products.

Cisco direct customers can access all of the above applications, in addition to the following:

➤ Pricing agent.
➤ Configuration agent.
➤ Order status.
➤ Invoice agent.
➤ Service order.
➤ Contract status.

Finally, resale partners can access all of these functions, plus they have the ability to check the lead times on Cisco products.

Users will get a different view of the site depending on who they are. Figure 3.1 shows the main page for CCO.

■ BENEFITS TO CUSTOMERS

Cisco lists the following benefits of CCO to its customers and resale partners:

➤ Providing unparalleled access to all of Cisco's critical business data.
➤ Delivering the ability to place orders online at any time, from anywhere in the world.
➤ Facilitating accurate configuration and order entry.

This last point has proven to be a significant benefit to customers. Before CCO, nearly 20 percent of orders submitted to Cisco, primarily by fax, were incorrectly configured or priced. Inaccuracies were usually discovered when a Cisco customer service representative was keying an order into Cisco's order-entry system running on an Oracle database.

Problems could be anything from a customer including incompatible versions of software in the order to omitting a required network component as mundane as a power cord. Under the old system, Cisco representatives would have to contact the customer to get the correct ordering information, then enter it into the database, sometimes causing delays in the ordering process of up to three days. And with lead times of up to four weeks for the most complex networking products, this kind of delay significantly impacted the user implementation.

Now, using the automated configuration system, which virtually ensures that customers cannot make mistakes when ordering products, CCO has shaved inaccurate orders down to less than 1 percent, saving both its customers and order management people time and ultimately money. Customers are able to get their networks installed faster and spend time working on more productive activities.

Cisco resale partners who are using the system say that it helps them deliver better service to their customers. For example, Brandi Ming, senior buyer at GE Capital Information Technology Solutions, which resells Cisco products to its Fortune 500 clients, said that using CCO helps reduce order time and get products to customers faster, which can be a competitive advantage. "It is definitely much more advanced than any manufacturer out there," said Ming, referring to Cisco's online ordering system. She said she particularly likes the ease of use of the system, its ability to track order status, and link to delivery services such as UPS to find out the status of a shipment.

Ming also says that because Cisco's product line is so complicated, having the online configuration capability reduces the amount of time GE sales representatives would otherwise have to spend working with a Cisco sales representative or local sales representative to place an order.

Other customers say they like CCO's online ordering system, citing benefits of saving time and improving productivity, but they want to find a way to integrate CCO with their existing ordering systems.

Cellular One, for example, started using CCO in earnest in early 1997. Charles Miano, a purchasing agent at Cell One, calls CCO a "vital tool" in the ordering process, providing Cell One administrative cost savings and improving the lead times of getting products delivered, as well as providing virtually error-free configuration of products ordered. All of these benefits help Cell One to be more productive, says Miano. However, Cell One currently uses Oracle Financials as its requisition software for purchases made with at least 20 vendors who supply products to the company.

"One of the things we're trying to work through (with Cisco) is integrating it with our current structure," says Miano. What Miano really likes about CCO is the configuration agent, the order status, and the online pricing. If someone at Cell One needs to order a Cisco product, they can go into the system, price and configure the product, then either submit the order if they're authorized or route it to an authorized purchasing agent like Miano. However, the information still needs to be keyed into the Oracle system and integrated with Cell One's financial database.

To solve this problem, Cell One is currently working on developing an intranet application that would link CCO to its financial database and current requisitioning system, providing more seamless integration. And Cisco, recognizing the problem that many of its large customers with multiple suppliers face, is now working on a solution to extend CCO to corporate intranets.

■ BENEFITS TO CISCO

Here's how CCO is benefiting Cisco:

➤ It's saving the company money by automating the ordering process.

➤ It has reduced by roughly 40 percent the amount of time that CSRs spend on ordering, freeing them up to focus on better service and relationship building [Cisco's corporate mantra].

➤ It provides a real example of how networking can be strategic to a company's business.

With just the cost savings alone, Cisco recouped the initial investment by a factor of 80 in the first year. For example, savings in literature and documentation shipping costs were $250 million through February 1997, demonstrating one of the key benefits to Cisco's networked commerce strategy. And while it certainly acknowledges the bottom line benefit, Cisco managers are even more adamant about what they see as the most important benefit of CCO: freeing up customer service representatives' and sales representatives' time to handle the big-picture and relationship issues. "We are developing a more highly skilled workforce," said Elizalde. "It is completely changing their jobs." For example, many former customer service representatives (reps) are now electronic commerce ambassadors, whose jobs are described later.

■ OVERCOMING RESISTANCE

While CCO users say they're happy with the system, Cisco did encounter some initial resistance to the online ordering system, primarily from resellers who didn't want the system to cannibalize their business, and also from Cisco sales representatives who had reservations about the system. On the reseller side, Cisco was acutely aware of its partners' concerns. "We would be going around them and creating channel conflict. That's not being a good sales partner," said Sinton. Nor would that have been good business strategy, considering that 70 percent of Cisco's revenues come through its resellers. Cisco's mission was to create a Web commerce site that would facilitate order entry for customers while protecting its resellers.

"On the salesforce side, there were two concerns," said Elizalde. It's no surprise what their No. 1 issue was: How is this going to affect my commissions? Cisco's sales representatives worried that if customers had access to the online ordering system, they could bypass the representatives. They were also worried that automation would reduce or even eliminate the human element, which could affect the sales and service function. Finally, sales representatives were concerned that customers would not use the system correctly and mess up orders.

Cisco solved both problems by:

1. Listening to its constituents' concerns.
2. Creating a strategy to address those issues.
3. Building a system to handle the problems.
4. Educating its constituents.

➤ Listening and Responding

Finding out about potential resistance before creating a Web commerce system is probably one of the most important things a company can do to ensure success. When its resellers expressed reservations about CCO, Cisco responded with two strategies:

1. It solicited advice from the Networked Commerce Advisory Board (NCAB).
2. It was very careful to position CCO as a way for existing customers and resellers to order products, not as a new channel that would take away resellers' business. In addition, it created Partner Initiated Customer Access (PICA), which allows its resellers to give access to CCO to its end users at their discretion.

NCAB served two purposes. Not only were the resale partners and customers heavily involved in helping to create the strategy of the site, they were also involved in testing and evaluating the system during the development process, providing valuable input in terms of assessing which features were working. Unfortunately, some of this happened late in the game. "We were behind the eightball," acknowledged Aragon, noting that her team was at least half-way, if not three-quarters of the way, into development of the commerce agents before they started getting real input from NCAB. The team had built a prototype and rolled it out to some beta users in April 1996, only to find that it was way off the mark on certain features, such as the ability to route orders. "One of the things we needed to do better was upfront market valuation of what kinds of features and functionality should be included," said Aragon.

For example, in the alpha version of the online ordering agent, there was no mechanism for routing an order. So if users at a company were shopping for products but were not authorized to order them, as is often the case at big companies, they could price and configure online, but couldn't order online. Therefore, they'd have to find a way to get the information to the purchasing agent or other authorized party, who would have to duplicate efforts by going online, filling out the order form, and submitting it to Cisco. This was not a good system, as CCO's alpha testers immediately discovered. So a routing mechanism was built into the ordering agent, which allows unauthorized users to price and configure products then send the form electronically to the appropriate person.

Other problems or fixes included putting in a menu with checkboxes to note the status of the online ordering process and developing an easier to use navigational tool. "The navigation piece was really confusing," said Aragon. "We had to completely rethink how we navigated through the system."

After reworking many of these features and functions, Cisco was finally ready to roll out the commerce system in July 1996.

■ SPREADING THE WORD

The next hurdle was letting people know the online ordering system was there and teaching them how to use it. With an initial goal of driving 30 percent of its total business online within one year (it is now generating 60 percent online), Cisco had a big job to do. With a $1.5 million online marketing budget, Cisco used a combination of the following campaigns to create awareness of the site and get people to use it:

➤ Direct e-mail marketing.

➤ Customer incentives.

➤ Sales representative incentives.

➤ Customer advocacy initiatives.

On the direct marketing side, Cisco launched an e-mail campaign to its direct customers and resale partners once the site was operational. It sent users a message introducing the site and providing the URL, then followed up with more e-mail if the users went to the site. In addition, it offered users a discount off their service contract, if they used the site. The result of this promotion was 800 people visiting the site and 100 customers or resale partners placing orders online.

Cisco offered the first 100 sales representatives to register customers online a $500 bonus. It also promoted 10 customer service representatives to electronic commerce ambassadors, a new position whose purpose was to educate customers about using the online ordering system and make sure their first and subsequent experiences on the Web site were positive.

■ LESSONS

While CCO is definitely a Web commerce success story, Cisco stumbled a bit along the way and learned some valuable lessons in the development and implementation of its commerce site. Two main things it did wrong were:

1. It didn't get input from users early enough in development.
2. It underestimated the network requirements.

On the second point, Cisco noticed when tracking online usage that it was having some problems with retention. Customers who had been using the system began to drop off their ordering. To find out why, Cisco customer support representatives did some evaluations and found out that performance had begun to drop because the system wasn't equipped to deal with the high volume of transactions.

To solve the problem, Cisco cleaned up the code, ordered some bigger servers (Sun Enterprise 5000s), and began closer transaction monitoring to be more aware if this type of problem were to happen again.

Once the network was in better shape to handle performance, Cisco kicked off a retention program to educate customers about the improvements.

In addition to lessons learned the hard way, Cisco also found out from experience what strategies and considerations are important in developing a Web commerce site. Here are the tips that Sinton offers to business executives who are considering launching or improving their online business:

1. If you're not adding value for the customer, don't bother.

2. Know who your target audience is.

3. Combine traditional marketing and new media to promote the site.

■ FUTURE

When asked to talk about CCO's future, Sinton faces his marker board, bows his head, and spreads his arms upward in a big V. Then he launches into a discussion of things to come, but not before whipping out an Electronic Commerce Strategy presentation slide that illustrates the following: While 1996 and 1997 were about developing and fine tuning the commerce applications on the Web to augment Cisco's existing services, 1998 and beyond will be about developing new ways to reach existing audiences and eventually developing new services and even channels to reach new customer audiences.

Cisco's first objective is to expand access to its primary commerce applications across three platforms:

1. The Web.
2. Dial-in access from the desktop.
3. Corporate intranets.

While the first mechanism was putting these functions up on the Web, the second, rolled out in mid-1997, was to deliver a desktop application that provided a dial-in capability for customers without Web access. And finally, for its largest customers, Cisco plans to introduce custom commerce applications that sit inside their corporate intranet, further automating the ordering process by linking directly to Cisco's internal systems. This is the kind of system that will address the needs of companies like Cellular One, which want to utilize their intranets for automated purchasing but have many vendors to work with.

Cisco is also in the process of evaluating new software tools that are now on the market to automate some of the functions on which it has spent millions in-house. Whether at this stage it makes sense to switch to third-party software remains to be seen, but if there's a better, more economical way of evolving the system, Cisco will consider it.

In Part II, different solutions for automating Web commerce will be discussed, starting with low-cost, third-party providers to more expensive in-house solutions.

Part II
Putting the Pieces Together

Chapter 4

Space for Rent: Outsourcing Commerce

So you're ready to open an online business. Now what? For many businesses that have decided to sell products and services online, the idea of buying server hardware and software; developing the site in-house; and finding providers to host, maintain, and manage the site is often enough to get them to put the investment off. That's why many businesses, particularly those that are just beginning to explore Web commerce, are turning to commerce solutions offered by third-party providers that free them from the responsibilities and many of the costs associated with in-house site development.

These solutions, offered increasingly by telecommunications providers, Internet service providers, and online malls already in business on the Web, provide a low-cost, relatively easy way for small and medium-sized companies to set up commerce sites on the Web. Some of the solutions are not much more than product listings on an existing Web mall, while others include Web hosting, a unique domain name, store setup, transactional capabilities, security services, and site management. Involving minimum upfront investments between $500 and $2,500 and monthly fees from $25 to $1,000, third-party solutions are often a good way for businesses to start experimenting with Web commerce. Eventually, merchants may decide to sink money into software, hardware, and Web site ownership rather than merely renting space on someone else's mall or Web server, but until they do, working with third-party providers is a good way for businesses to start learning about Web commerce without making a significant upfront investment.

This chapter will look at a sampling of entry-level commerce solutions from the following types of providers:

> Internet malls.
> Telecommunications companies.
> Internet service providers.

■ INTERNET MALLS

At last count there were more than 3,000 malls in cyberspace. What constitutes a Web mall? Generally speaking, malls on the Internet are not unlike malls in the real world. They provide a place under one roof (or under one URL) where buyers can enter through a common front door and shop for products without having to drive from store to store. Usually, they provide a common payment structure, so consumers can buy from different stores on one credit card or using some other payment form. For merchants, the malls provide the basic infrastructure, although some custom work to the inside of the store is still usually required to enable merchants to be commerce-ready. The mall management often provides other benefits such as marketing and advertising.

There are malls for vertical markets, such as Golf Mall USA (www.golf-mall.com) and Car Mall (www.car-mall.com). There are regional malls, such as the South Florida Mall (www.sf-mall.com) and the Laguna Hills Mall (www.n-sale .com/malls/lagunahills). There are special interest and lifestyle malls, such as the disABILITY Mall (www.rvlscore

.org/mall/index.html) and The Rainbow Mall (www
.rainbow-mall.com) for gay and lesbian resources.

Some malls, such as The Internet Mall, provide free listing services for merchants, while others, such as Choice
Mall, charge an upfront fee to build sites for merchants, and
a monthly fee to maintain and manage storefronts. There
are pros and cons to putting your store in an online mall.
Here are some of the pros:

➤ Usually lower upfront costs than stand-alone stores.
➤ Built-in site traffic.
➤ Broader advertising and marketing.
➤ Frees merchant from hosting and managing site.

On the con side, merchants may want to consider the
following:

➤ Loss of autonomy.
➤ Usually income sharing with mall operator.
➤ Limitations imposed by mall operator.

Some merchants may find it makes more sense to buy
their own storefront software, which starts at around $1,500,
and be responsible for their own site. For more information
on merchant and storefront software, see Chapter 5.

The next section will look at the services offered by one
of the largest malls on the Internet, Choice Mall.

➤ From Infomercials to the Internet

Choice Mall (www.choicemall.com) is owned and operated by
Guthy-Renker Internet, a subsidiary of Guthy-Renker, a $400
million company that produces TV infomercials (Figure 4.1).
Launched in November 1995, Choice Mall now represents
more than 1,500 merchants, in categories spanning fashion,
kids products, home items, gifts, travel, and other products
and services. Partnering with technology companies such as

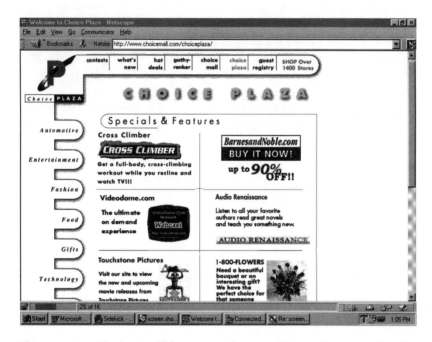

Figure 4.1. Choice Mall has more than 1,500 merchants on its site, selling everything from fitness to flowers.

Netscape, InfoSeek, RealTime Media, and Hot Coupons, Choice Mall offers searching, multimedia, transaction processing, and other capabilities to its merchants. The mall is now getting more than 8 million hits per month, providing shoppers with the ability to search through 18 categories of items in 70 regional locations. Choice Mall is targeted at small to medium-sized businesses that want to put up electronic storefronts but don't have the resources in-house to do so. For a setup fee of $1,695 for a two-page Web site or $2,995 for a five-page Web site, merchants get a package that includes Web site development, space on the mall, order processing, and secure transactional capabilities from the Web server to the merchant location. And for around $25 a month, Choice Mall provides hosting and maintenance services.

As part of the help provided with setting up their site, merchants receive a two-day interactive training seminar, which provides information on effective ways to set up and market a Web site, write compelling content, and run a successful online business. But the biggest advantage to putting up a storefront in Choice Mall, says the company, is tapping into Guthy-Renker's national advertising program, which includes approximately $100 million spent yearly on television advertising alone, that helps drive traffic to the Web site. "People are spending $30,000 to $40,000 developing Web sites, but they're not getting any business," said Kenneth Burke, vice president of development at Guthy-Renker Internet, which sells $1 million worth of its own products online yearly, including its flagship product Power Rider exerciser, Perfect Smile teeth whitening system, and Personal Power skin care program. "Marketing is everything," said Burke.

Small businesses that have ventured down the Web commerce path have found truth in this. Remember Eddie Lloyd from Horizon Tours (Chapter 2)? He didn't spend a lot of money on his Web site, but he sat around for days waiting for people to find him. Eventually he listed his site with search engines and travel-related sites, but it was all on his own time. One of the advantages to signing up with a nationally advertised mall is exposure to all those eyeballs. Choice Mall also has partnerships with C/Net, Talk City, and TheGlobe.com for mall position on their sites. On a cost scale, the upfront price of Web site development on Choice Mall is about half the price of low-end merchant server or catalog software (such as those offered by iCat, Microsoft, and Intershop). The technical expertise required for the mall setup is virtually nil, because Guthy-Renker uses its own Web developers to build the site with HTML programming. Plus, if you're going to be buying merchant server or catalog building software, you still need hardware to run it on, more technical know-how, and you need to arrange for your own hosting and maintenance, which will probably cost you more than $25 a month.

However, catalog software gives merchants much more flexibility and sophistication than being in an online mall, so if you have more than thousands of products or want to build in features such as dynamic page generation, a mall might not be the best place for your online business.

But for mom-and-pop shops or even bigger businesses that have limited resources and don't want to spend much money or time developing their Web site (the average implementation for Choice Mall merchants is two to three weeks) the mall solution might be a good way to start evaluating whether Web commerce has any potential for their business. For information, Choice Mall, 3340 Ocean Park Blvd., 2nd Floor, Santa Monica, CA 90405, (800) 970-5999, www.choicemall.com.

➤ Mall Merchant: Shiatsu Shower Mats

Gary Heller, who lives in Honolulu, is the inventor of a product called the Shiatsu Shower Mat™, which applies acupressure to zones on the soles of the feet through nodules on the mat for therapeutic purposes. Heller developed the product and was ready to start selling it in 1996 although he did not yet have any distribution channels. His business partner, Bob DeCamp, had been exploring the Internet and proposed opening up an electronic storefront in a shared server environment at an Internet service provider. But Heller and De-Camp were not convinced that would be the best solution. Although they could lease space on a server for as little as $25 a month, they were still looking at doing their own site development, including the ability to process credit card orders, and conduct their own marketing.

"It's great to have your name on a server, but if you're on a no-name server, how is anyone going to find you?" said Heller. During the company's search for an Internet outlet, Guthy-Renker came to town with a workshop on the Internet. Heller and DeCamp went, bringing along their financial advisor, and they were sold on the potential of setting up a shop on Choice Mall. "It gets down to exposure," said Heller. "We knew the clout they had on TV (with infomercials). Advertising is everything."

So Shiatsu Shower Mats signed up for Guthy-Renker's five-page Web site package at a cost of roughly $2,500. Because they were one of the early merchants on Choice Mall, they got a deal on the monthly hosting rate, paying only $10 a month. The package included site development, order processing, Web site hosting and maintenance, and most importantly, national advertising.

In the first year, Shiatsu Shower Mats more than recouped its one-time investment of $2,500 through online orders of the mats, which sell for $14.95 plus $5 for shipping and handling. (That's about 166 mats.) The company benefited from having a unique product that Guthy-Renker used as an example during its traveling road show to sign up business. However, even without the endorsement of Guthy-Renker, the mat was doing well enough on its own just by being in Choice Mall.

For example, the editor of *Massage Magazine* saw the product while surfing the Net and wrote an article about it, resulting in about 50 orders. The owner of Great American Backrub, a retail chain of massage services and products, saw the mats while on the Web, and placed an order for 12 cases to sell in its 15 stores.

The biggest break for Shiatsu Shower Mats came in May 1997, when a writer for *The New York Times* saw the product in Choice Mall while looking for products to review and featured the mat in a prominent article about high-tech shower products. Within days, the company sold more than 1,000 mats as a result of the exposure, generating revenue of more than $15,000, or six times the amount of its initial investment!

Now, Heller is getting into custom design work for clients across the country, from hotels to sports associations, in which he'll incorporate logos and brands into the acupressure nodules on the mats. His business is booming, and he's convinced that being in the mall with its national exposure, including TV advertising, is responsible. For now, he plans to stick with Choice Mall, although he's not sure what will happen in the future as his business grows. Here's what he says about his Web commerce experience:

> *If your bottom line can afford it, you need to get on the Internet because of the learning experience. However,*

with all of the Internet hype, don't be disappointed. As an entrepreneur or a business owner, you have to remember that this is just one piece of your pie. You are really publishing something. You need to keep it fresh and updated, and put it (promotional information such as the URL) on everything you have: Business cards, letter heads, correspondence, etc. The important thing is to start your learning curve now, get your toe wet, and get advertising. Then your orders will start growing.

■ TELECOMMUNICATIONS COMPANIES

Telecommunications providers, which started out offering Internet connectivity and Web site hosting as a natural extension of their communications business, have increasingly been offering more complete commerce solutions to their business customers. Here's a look at what the big three long-distance companies are offering in the way of commerce services.

➤ AT&T's Web Services

AT&T launched Easy World Wide Web (EW3) in April 1996, which provides small and medium-sized businesses with Web development tools, a hosting environment, training, support, and other services necessary to set up sites on the Web. EW3 is priced at $295 a month for existing AT&T long-distance customers and $395 a month for non-AT&T customers, plus a one-time registration fee of $1,000. Monthly hosting includes 100 MB of server storage space and 200 MB of data transfers by site visitors. For perspective, 200 MB translates to roughly 37,000 printed document pages (with each byte representing one character). For more than 200 MB of data downloaded per month, AT&T charges additional fees, starting at $155 a month for between 200 and 500 MB, and up to $1,500 a month for between 3,500 and 7,000 MB.

The high end represents the amount of data that could be stored on about a dozen CD-ROMs, such as graphically rich encyclopedic data. For businesses that have graphic intensive sites and expect to do high volumes of data transfer, AT&T has Enhanced Web Site Development, which includes more custom development and features such as load sharing.

In October 1996, AT&T rolled out SecureBuy, which added secure credit card processing capabilities to its customers' Web sites. SecureBuy is priced at $395 a month for existing AT&T long distance customers and $495 a month for non-AT&T customers, plus a one-time registration fee of $500. The first 500 transactions are free, after which AT&T charges $2 per transaction for its existing long-distance customers and $3 per transaction for noncustomers.

Integrated with OM-Transact software from Open Market Inc., SecureBuy provides the following capabilities:

➤ Order acceptance and tracking.
➤ Credit card authorization and processing through links into financial processing networks.
➤ Sales tax and shipping charge calculation.
➤ Digital receipts for customers.
➤ Management reports for merchants.

In addition, SecureBuy comes with a catalog wizard that works in conjunction with Microsoft FrontPage to help merchants set up their online stores. At AT&T training classes, merchants learn how to work with the software to create their electronic storefronts. Security is provided through encryption, secure socket layer (SSL) technology, and firewall protection. For a more thorough discussion of security, see Chapter 8.

AT&T pitches SecureBuy as a solution that requires no capital investment upfront, which can be important to businesses that worry about investing in technology that might become obsolete. "All the complexity is taken out with the AT&T network," said Keith Olson, director of new channel development at AT&T. "Our brand says it's always going to work, it's nonstop, it's backed up with service guarantees, and it's all available today."

One service guarantee that AT&T offers with SecureBuy is its "Never Miss an Order" program, in which it guarantees its merchants credit for any orders that might be lost over the Internet. In addition, consumers who use AT&T Universal cards to charge items bought on the Internet can safeguard their online purchases up to $50 per order.

AT&T continues to expand its service offerings through alliances with a variety of strategic partners. In March 1997, for example, it formed a marketing alliance with Wells Fargo to provide a one-stop Internet commerce solution for both companies' customers, including Internet commerce and credit card processing through Wells Fargo, and Web site hosting, catalog creation, and transaction processing services from AT&T. There are no additional charges for these services. However, neither company is limiting itself to either provider. AT&T will work with other banks for credit card processing, while Wells Fargo will work with other telecom providers. The agreement is just one example of the many ways in which specialty providers are teaming up to provide end-to-end commerce solutions to customers. In March 1998, AT&T rolled out AT&T eCommerce Suite, which includes EW3, SecureBuy, Interactive Answers, and a Business Assist program for $695 per month with a one-time fee of $500. For information: AT&T, 32 Avenue of the Americas, New York, NY 10013, (800) 7HOSTIN, www.att.com.

➤ MCI Web Commerce

Like many other companies that have been playing in the Internet space for years, MCI has shifted its Web commerce strategy as the Internet has evolved. MCI was an electronic mall pioneer, launching marketplaceMCI in late 1994, aimed at small to medium-sized businesses that wanted to set up electronic storefronts. At its peak, the mall had between 30 and 100 merchants, but MCI shut down the mall in early 1996.

The primary reason MCI got out of the mall business was a decision to align with Microsoft Corp. and the software giant's Microsoft Network online service rather than with News Corp. and its I-guide online service, which MCI initially had partnered with in an effort to drive traffic to marketplaceMCI. "We decided we did not want to be in the online content business, and Microsoft was a good partner," said David Samuels, product manager for MCI Web Commerce. Under its agreement with Microsoft, announced in January 1996, MCI said it would market a customized version of MSN called "MSN from MCI," an online service that provides Internet access via MCI's Internet network, Microsoft Network content and communities, information on the World Wide Web, as well as MCI customized content and other services to its customers. However, during its experience as a mall operator, MCI learned a valuable lesson: Customers often want more flexibility than mall operators are able to deliver. In addition to wanting flexibility with site design, customers also wanted more flexibility with regard to financial transactions. MarketplaceMCI ran on Netscape Commerce Server and was connected to one credit card processing network, First Data Corp. (FDC). But many of its merchant customers wanted to set up accounts with their existing banks, which often offered more favorable terms than FDC, and MCI was not able to set up accounts with all of these banks. "As a service provider, you have to respect your customers' existing relationships," said Samuels. While it had always intended to offer Web commerce services, although not necessarily in a mall environment, MCI grew its Web commerce strategy to include Internet, intranet, and extranet environments. Now, rather than targeting just small businesses, MCI is also targeting Fortune 2000 and larger companies that don't need as much handholding. For businesses that do not yet have a commerce-enabled Web site, MCI offers MCI Web-Commerce, for a monthly rate of $500, that is integrated with OM-Transact from Open Market and Microsoft Merchant Server. It provides the following capabilities:

➤ Order processing and tracking.

➤ Credit card authorization and processing through links into First USA and FDC.

➤ Sales tax and shipping charge calculation.

➤ Invoice reporting.

➤ Management reports.

WebCommerce also comes with Microsoft FrontPage, in addition to an online manual that helps customers set up digital offers to commerce-enable their sites. It also provides access and instructions to a common gateway interface (CGI) library that customers can use to generate either static or dynamic storefronts.

If customers need further help with Web site development, MCI will refer them to Web design partners. With WebCommerce, MCI is targeting companies that expect to do a good deal of business on their Web sites and want to take advantage of MCI's fixed flat rates rather than entry-level rates offered by competitors such as AT&T (starting at $295 a month for hosting). The trade-off is that MCI charges no additional fees for transactions or data downloads. In addition to providing a Web commerce solution, MCI offers the following hosting environments for its customers:

➤ Alpha Hosting, which does not support commerce, priced at $500 a month.

➤ Premium Hosting, a shared server environment, priced at a flat rate of $1,000 a month, for unlimited transactions and downloads.

➤ Custom Hosting, a dedicated server environment, priced depending on server storage needs and bandwidth. The average custom hosting customer spends between $3,000 and $5,000 a month.

➤ MCI High-End Customer: Universal Press Syndicate

Universal Press Syndicate, a Kansas City, Missouri, company whose main business is syndicating comic strips to newspapers, was looking for a way to conduct commerce on the Web in early 1996. It explored a shared server hosting environment such as the kind offered by ISPs and telecommunications providers, but decided in the end that it wanted to own its own servers, but place them in someone else's facilities for managing. "We didn't want to be limited to the bandwidth constraints we'd have if we hosted our servers in-house," said Chris Pizey, webmaster at Universal Press. For example, if the company had high traffic on its site and wanted to switch its connection from a T-1 line to a T-3 line, it might have to wait for between 30 and 60 days for the telecommunications provider to make the switch. "That is not a positive thing," said Pizey, pointing to traffic of 1 million hits per day the business is now getting at its three major Web sites:

- ➤ www.uexpress.com, for most of Universal Press' syndicated content.
- ➤ www.garfield.com, for Garfield brand comics, mugs, calendars, and other products.
- ➤ www.uclick.com, which provides custom content to online newspapers.

After evaluating hosting services offered by AT&T, Universal Press Syndicate's existing long-distance provider and competitor MCI, UPS decided to go with MCI because it offered the custom hosting environment, in which UPS could own its own servers while MCI managed them, and also because of marketplaceMCI, which provided a way for UPS to conduct commerce from its site, while at the time AT&T did not.

However, Pizey said, "We signed onto marketplaceMCI, but we didn't really care about the mall. We just wanted commerce. We didn't want to monkey around with setting up the shopping ourselves and deal with credit cards." With marketplaceMCI, UPS was freed from having to handle the electronic storefront setup and credit card processing.

When MCI trashed the mall concept and started offering WebCommerce, Universal Press became a beta customer for the new service. One of the big differences with WebCommerce was the integration with Open Market's OM-Transact software, which lets merchants design their own pages in-house and send just the customer order to the OM transaction processing software running on MCI's servers. Before, with marketplaceMCI, if any content changes were made to merchants' storefronts, they had to be uploaded to MCI's server, which was a Netscape Commerce Server, and UPS found this to be a limitation.

"Now, we have the ability to design our own pages, and we just have to embed the digital offer," said Pizer. For UPS, which has a staff of programmers who are used to doing CGI programming, embedding the digital offers is not a big deal. The staff designs its own pages using HTML programming. In addition, UPS works with a Web developer, McLean, Virginia, based Proxicom, which helped with the overall strategy, design, and content presentation for the sites, which eventually cost hundreds of thousands of dollars. That included the purchase of two Silicon Graphics Inc. Challenge S servers, which were priced at about $30,000 each and came bundled with Netscape Commerce Server software, as well as fees paid to the Web developer and to UPS' own internal technical staff. And UPS also paid thousands of dollars a month in Web hosting fees to MCI, although Pizer wouldn't be specific.

So far, Universal Press Syndicate has not seen a return on its Web investment. It processes about six orders a day for merchandise such as mugs, calendars, and greeting cards. However, Pizer said that it expects its business to take off in the next year as it launches a more aggressive marketing campaign that will include being listed on search engine sites, online shopping malls, as well as promoting the URL in comic strips and other merchandise, and as people become more comfortable shopping on the Web.

➤ Sprint

Sprint, which competes with AT&T and MCI in the long distance market, is also ramping up its Internet services, although it is now offering access, security, dialup Internet, and connectivity rather than packaged commerce services. One of Sprint's commerce initiatives is managed firewall services, which lets companies outsource the management of a secure firewall between their Web site and internal databases. For a more thorough discussion of security, see Chapter 8. Sprint also offers IP Web Hosting, with a 100 percent site availability guarantee to make sure your site is up 24 × 7 (that's 24 hours a day, 7 days a week).

In addition to offering managed firewall services, Sprint also offers a separate intranet backbone for companies that are conducting secure transactions on private TCP/IP networks. For information: Sprint Corp., 2330 Shawnee Mission Pkwy., Westwood, KS 66205, (800) 816-7325, www.sprint.com.

■ INTERNET SERVICE PROVIDERS

Internet service providers, which traditionally provide Internet access, Web site hosting, and other Internet services, are beginning to offer some commerce solutions for their existing and potential new customers. With increasing competition from telecommunications providers, upstart and established Web development companies, computer firms, and other technology companies, ISPs recognize that they have to continually expand their service offerings to meet their clients' needs, and those needs are increasingly including commerce. While most of the big ISPs are still focused mainly on providing secure hosting environments that support electronic commerce transactions, some are aggressively moving into commerce services by partnering with payment providers, merchant server developers, and other third parties to serve their business partners' needs. Here are a few examples of the types of services and strategies that have been rolled out by a few of the nation's largest ISPs.

➤ UUNet

UUNet, based in Fairfax, Virginia, is one of the oldest ISPs in North America. In 1997, UUNet formed a subsidiary for Web services and coined the term *Web service provider,* aiming to be the leader in secure Web hosting, according to Paul Hoffman, manager of Web product marketing and developing at UUNet. To that end, UUNet has formed partnerships with electronic payment provider CyberCash and with computer software firm Microsoft Corp., which develops Microsoft Site Server, to provide its clients with electronic catalog presentation capabilities using Site Server, and secure transactional capabilities using CyberCash's electronic payment solutions on their Web sites. Priced starting at about $300 a month, UUNet's secure transaction and hosting services let merchants process both electronic cash and credit card payments from their sites. As a result of its merger with ANS in January 1998, UUNet is now offering additional commerce capabilities using Open Market and iCat software. For information: UUNet Technologies Inc., 3060 Williams Dr., Fairfax, VA 22031-4648, (800) 4UU-NET4, www.uu.net.

➤ TCG CERFnet

One of the established commercial ISPs, San Diego-based CERFnet, which was acquired in 1996 by alternate telecommunications provider Teleport Communications Group, has built its reputation on network reliability. "If it's not reliable, none of this works," says Pushpendra Mohta, executive vice president of CERFnet. CERFnet, like UUnet, offers secure transactional capabilities through partnerships with Cy-berCash and other software providers, and utilizes Netscape Commerce server for secure communications. CERFnet is relying on third-party providers such as Microsoft and other software companies for commerce solutions. "For Web commerce to take off, people have to enable the small merchants," said Mohta, pointing to solutions such as shared merchant servers that will give merchants a way to launch Web commerce operations without making signifi-cant investments in hardware and software. Once they have merchant server capabilities in place, CERFnet will provide the secure hosting and network connection ser-vices, starting at about $250 a month. For information: CERFnet, 9805 Scranton Rd., San Diego, CA 92121, (888) CERFNET, www.cerf.net.

➤ BBN Planet

BBN Planet Corp., Cambridge, Massachusetts, has been pro-viding networking services for more than 25 years, helping to build ARPANET, the precursor to the Internet, beginning in 1969. Caught up in the acquisition wave of telecommuni-cations providers as they try to broaden their services, BBN was bought in 1997 by GTE. BBN Planet focuses its electronic commerce services on providing a secure hosting and con-nectivity environment for electronic transactions, although it did play in the transaction arena for a short time by offer-ing a service called Merchant Advantage, which provided businesses with tools to design and operate commercial Web sites. However, BBN is no longer offering Merchant Advan-tage, instead concentrating on its secure network services, such as its Internet Site Patrol managed Internet security services and Web Advantage server co-location and content-design services. It also offers custom solutions for customers, such as the application discussed next for the Massachusetts Registry of Motor Vehicles. For information: BBN Planet Corp., 150 Cambridge Park Dr., Cambridge, MA 02140, (800) 472-4565, www.bbn.com.

➤ BBN Provides Secure Transactions for Massachusetts RMV

The Massachusetts Registry of Motor Vehicles, based in Boston, was a government pioneer in Web commerce, becoming the first state motor vehicle department to provide a way for users to register vehicles, pay fines, and buy items such as specialty plates on the Internet. When planning the strategy for its commerce site, key information systems personnel at the RMV began talking to the Massachusetts Information Technologies Division (ITD), which is the MIS department for the state, supporting clients such as the Massachusetts Department of Revenue and smaller agencies such as parks. The two divisions decided to work on a joint project to set up a Web commerce site, which eventually would be used to collect revenue for fishing licenses, state park permits, and other state services, although initially the project would focus on motor vehicle registration. The goal was to serve state residents better by eliminating the time and expense involved in obtaining licenses and processing other requests, as well as to make the department more efficient. However, said Larry McConnell, director of information services for the Massachusetts RMV, "Neither one of us had people on staff that understood commerce Internet transactions. We just knew that we wanted the transactions to be secure." So the state issued a request for proposals, and narrowed down the field to two candidates: Software company Oracle Corp., whose bid was in the hundreds of thousands of dollars, and BBN Planet, whose bid was about $50,000. The fees included developing a total solution for secure electronic transactions, integrating with the RMV's existing mainframe, and providing a hosting environment. However, Oracle's bid included more sophisticated system features such as transaction tunneling, which would provide secure end-to-end transactions from the Web browser into the RMV mainframe and back. RMV decided the Oracle solution was too expensive and opted for the BBN solution, which included secure transactions from the user's browser into the RMV server hosted by BBN. Rather than providing a secure link into RMV's mainframe for real-time transaction processing, the Web server would retrieve data nightly from batch transactions being downloaded from the mainframe, which holds driver record, licensing, registration, and other information.

McConnell said one of the biggest pluses to BBN's secure Internet commerce service was the level of custom work the ISP provided. RMV staffers held a series of meetings with BBN developers, during which they explained how they wanted the transactions to flow, what information they wanted on the screens, what screens they wanted the user to see, and other design elements. BBN did the rest, including developing the content presentation, transactional capabilities, and process flow using CGI scripts and other programming. The main commerce features on the site allow users to do the following:

1. Pay traffic fines.
2. Renew vehicle registration.
3. Order vanity plates.

The RMV says it's on its way to recouping the investment in the site: In 1996, it generated $690,000 in transactions, mainly in vehicle registration renewals. Although this is not a new revenue stream, the cost savings are significant in terms of RMV resources. "One of the main benefits," said McConnell, "is in public relations. People just see the government in a different light when they see the government taking strides to keep up with current technology."

■ BEYOND ISPs

While most ISPs provide an environment in which to conduct secure electronic commerce, most still require clients to development their own sites. That's why many businesses are turning to outside parties to provide not only Web hosting but site development, strategy, marketing, and other services. Many of these Web development companies, which number in the tens of thousands, are true full-service Internet providers, while others specialize in backend database integration, virtual reality development, building communities of interest, and other areas. Web site development can be cheap, particularly if a company requires a bare-bones site and just wants a programmer to do some HTML pages. These consulting and programming services can cost as little as $25 to $50 an hour.

However, for a full-blown development effort, including commerce strategy, site development, and ongoing maintenance, companies can expect to spend anywhere from $10,000 to millions of dollars. For these services, they're turning to systems integrators, consultants, and Web development firms. A good source for finding Web developers is *Advertising Age*'s "Web Developer Directory" on its Business Marketing Web site (www.netb2b.com).

Chapter 5

Electronic Catalog and Merchant Server Software

Many businesses that want to launch Web commerce operations for both business-to-consumer and business-to-business models are making the decision to buy their own merchant server or electronic catalog software to run in-house. These solutions, priced from $1,500 to $100,000 or more, depending on the level of sophistication and customization required, are suited for businesses with some of the following characteristics:

➤ Currently selling products in a retail environment.

➤ Have an existing paper or electronic catalog operation.

➤ Sell Internet services, such as Internet hosting, design, and connectivity.

➤ Want to own the hardware and software for Web commerce.

➤ Desire more flexibility and control than third-party providers can offer.

➤ Do not have products or services that require complex pricing or configuration processing.

➤ Do not have complex database integration requirements.

➤ Have some technical resources in-house to set up the software.

Businesses that choose to buy merchant server or electronic catalog software need to have hardware to run it on, which usually means at least a Windows NT or a Unix operating system environment, as well as Web server software and a hosting and Internet connectivity environment. Targeting merchants themselves as well as Internet service providers, electronic catalog software is rapidly becoming an easy, affordable way for businesses to set up a Web commerce presence. Nonprofit organizations to Fortune 500 companies are implementing these types of solutions to sell goods online, and they're finding that electronic catalogs can be an efficient way to conduct business online. There are dozens of storefront software packages on the market. Some of the leaders in this niche include Microsoft, IBM, iCat, Intershop, and The Internet Factory, all of which provide electronic catalog solutions targeting small to large companies, including telecommunications companies and ISPs that lease storefronts to merchants for hundreds of dollars a month and up. Packaged catalog solutions typically include the following features:

➤ Electronic store setup.

➤ Product presentation.

➤ Order processing.

➤ Payment processing.

➤ Support for third-party software such as shipping and tax calculation packages.

Some of the major electronic catalog solutions, including their positioning, target market, differentiating features, pricing, and strategies for the future are discussed next.

■ INTERNET FACTORY

The Internet Factory, based in Pleasanton, California, offers electronic commerce software for ISPs, through which retailers can lease electronic storefronts for a suggested monthly price of between $100 and $500.

The Internet Factory offers both single-store software (called Merchant Builder 2.2, priced at $6,995 for three store licenses) and mall commerce software, priced starting at $10,000. In early 1998, the Internet Factory released Merchant Builder 3.0 to target ISPs. "A lot of people are standardizing on other servers," said John Murray, vice president of marketing for the Internet Factory. "Our goal is to pre-integrate with the major solutions."

Merchant Builder 3.0 allows ISPs to offer low-cost, full-featured storefronts to new and existing Web hosting customers. It includes the following features:

➤ *Store creation and management tools:* Using wizards and forms, merchants can create and test Web stores without ISP assistance. These stores then can be converted to paid stores at the end of the trial period.

➤ *Store templates:* Supporting NetObjects Fusion 3.0, Microsoft FrontPage, Netscape Composer, and other standard Web site editors, Merchant Builder lets businesses create Web sites without programming.

➤ *Support for multiple database products:* Merchant Builder runs on high performance database servers from Microsoft, Oracle, Sybase, and others.

➤ *Tools to manage merchant stores:* Store building and maintenance wizards, sales and sales tax reports, order tracking, credit card authorization, shipping and handling, and sales tax calculations all are included.

Retail pricing will depend on terms negotiated with ISPs.

Since one of the key costs associated with electronic storefront operations is telecommunications service, which can be priced at $1,000 a month and up for high-speed connections (such as T-1 lines that provide data transfer speeds of 1.54 MBs), smaller retail operations might want to consider going with ISPs that offer catalog solutions from companies such as the Internet Factory and others that will roll the connectivity charges into a monthly price and include all of the functionality of a single store environment. However, businesses that already have telecommunications lines and IS infrastructure in place might want to consider investing in their own software.

"For someone who is very knowledgeable about their products and doesn't have to buy a box or a T-1 line, it's a small incremental cost," says Murray. Merchant Builder customers include Harley Davidson, Cyber Shop, and others. For information: The Internet Factory, 6654 Koll Center Pkwy., Suite 150, Pleasanton, CA 94566, (650) 559-9000, www.ifact.com.

■ ICAT

iCat Corp., in business since 1993, is considered one of the market leaders in electronic storefront software, with clients ranging from Guess Jeans to the Kentucky Derby. It provides a free Web store through its iCat Commerce Online for merchants with up to 10 items; $49.95 a month for up to 50 items; $99 a month for up to 100 items; and $350 a month for up to 3,000 items. For merchants who want to own the software, iCat's Electronic Commerce Suite software is priced starting at $3,495 for the Standard Edition and $9,995 for the Professional Edition, and is targeted at small to large merchants as well as ISPs and other third-party providers. (See Figure 5.1.)

"We long ago gave up having a target market," said Craig Danuloff, president and chief executive officer of iCat, based in Seattle. "Electronic catalogs, like the telephone, apply to all businesses, whether you're selling cars or vacations, low-tech or high-tech goods."

Figure 5.1. iCat catalog software lets merchants set up shop on the Web for as little as $3,500.

iCat's Standard Edition software is designed for merchants that do not require highly customized or sophisticated catalogs that require interfaces with different databases. Standard Edition includes the following features:

➤ Ready-to-use catalog templates for store setup.

➤ Shopping cart functionality.

➤ Product and feature searching.

➤ Cross-selling.

➤ Secure payment processing.

"If you're going to use built-in templates, you use Standard," said Danuloff. "If you want to customize it and learn how to develop tools to build a sophisticated catalog, use Professional." With iCat's Standard edition, "We wanted to give people on limited budgets, or those who are not sure how serious they are, to have an affordable way to set up electronic commerce." Currently, iCat Standard Edition runs on the Windows NT operating system. For more serious developers, including experienced merchants, ISPs, and Web developers, with more sophisticated system needs, Professional Edition includes the following features:

➤ Support for high-end ODBC databases.

➤ ISAPI (Information Server Application Programming Interface) and NSAPI (Netscape Server Application Programming Interface) interfaces, to run on Microsoft and Netscape servers.

➤ Options for third-party plug-ins such as shipping and tax calculation software.

➤ Visual command language editor.

➤ Provision of source code.

iCat's Professional Edition runs in the Unix operating environment. For information: iCat Corp., 1420 Fifth Ave., Suite 1800, Seattle, WA 98101-2333, (206) 505-8800, www.icat.com.

■ INTERSHOP

Intershop Communications, based in Burlingame, California, offers catalog solutions targeted at both merchants and mall operators such as ISPs. Its merchant edition, Intershop 3, introduced in April 1998, is priced starting at $4,995 for a single-store solution, with additional charges for multiple licenses. Intershop, which started out as NetConsult Communications Inc., has been in business since 1992 and specializes in back-end database integration. It counts among its clients small businesses such as Softwear.com, which sells neckties online, and large corporations such as Hewlett-Packard Europe, which utilizes Intershop software to sell business-to-business products and integrate with backend inventory systems and corporate databases.

However, while Intershop had been targeting businesses that wanted to set up stand-alone operations with the Intershop Online product, with Intershop 3, it is betting heavily on the ISP model. "The majority of electronic storefronts will end up at ISPs," said Stephan Schambach, president and chief executive officer of Intershop. "It's much more cost effective," he adds, noting that large ISPs and telecommunications providers can offer more reliable service, better performance, and higher security than individual companies setting up electronic commerce operations. "A large ISP or telecommunications company can do it much better than you can do it in-house," said Schambach. "It's much cheaper, and the cost per store is lower than if you have a dedicated machine."

In addition, he added, "If you do it in-house, you have to have know-how on how to set up a firewall, if you want to have a secure environment." Particularly for companies that are integrating their Web storefront with backend databases containing sensitive data such as customer account information or financial data, firewall protection is especially critical. For a more thorough discussion of security issues, see Chapter 8.

Intershop 3 offers the following editions:

➤ Merchant edition, for a single store license, includes a full set of store creation and business management tools.

➤ Hosting edition, targeted at ISPs, and thousands of stores.

➤ Developer edition, targeted at Web developers and designers.

Intershop 3 features include the following:

1. Site Administration Module to manage multiple stores.
2. Integration with third-party applications and data-bases.
3. User-defined template language extensions, to let customers create values for colors, images, banners, and so forth, to apply to all templates in a store.
4. SSL security.

For information: Intershop Communications Inc., 111 Anza Blvd., Suite 205, Burlingame, CA 94010, (800) 736-5197, www.intershop.com.

■ CATALOG USER IMPLEMENTATION: ICAT DEVELOPER

Global Interactive Systems Inc. is a Louisville, Kentucky, Web development firm that uses iCat, as well as other catalog packages, to build electronic storefronts for its clients, including ISPs and individual merchants. For example, Global Interactive is building an online mall for Charter Communications, an Atlanta-based Internet service provider, which plans to lease storefront space to businesses for between $250 and $500 a month.

"A common rule with ISPs is, they're not making nearly what they should be," said Jason Heffran, vice president, electronic commerce, at GIS. "With this model, ISPs can get additional revenues from existing clients," he adds.

GIS, which has agreements with iCat, Intershop, and other specialized software companies, builds complete electronic storefronts for clients, integrating off-the-shelf software with backend databases and other customizable features.

"iCat will fit 99 percent of problems that companies have facing e-commerce, and fit within 85–95 percent of budgets," said Heffran. However, he said, companies looking at implementing electronic catalog software should expect to double the price they pay just in labor costs for developing the system.

That's where Web developers such as GIS come in. GIS will work with clients to do the electronic storefront setup, as well as integration with backend databases, for fees ranging from $15,000 to $40,000 or higher.

GIS targets companies that typically generate less than $3 million in revenue and are just starting out with electronic commerce. "They have money, but they don't have the type of money to gamble $60,000 to $70,000 on a standalone, fully integrated commerce solution. They want to take baby steps," said Heffran.

Global Interactive's strategy is to work with clients to determine how they can implement electronic commerce software not only to generate revenue but to save costs associated with selling goods and distributing other information electronically.

GIS conducts feasibility studies for clients and targets where they can save money on costs associated with processing transactions such as taking orders in a call center or sending faxes confirming orders. "We look at where they are not taking advantage of technology, and price the project to recoup expenses within 9 to 14 months," said Heffran. For example, by automating the sale of goods and services using electronic storefront software, a company might be able to eliminate the job of a customer service representative, who might be making an annual salary of $34,000. Or, it could cut overall costs associated with an 800-call center by automating part of the sales cycle over the Web.

In addition to building sites for clients, GIS has developed its own online store, called the Stadium Shop at www .stadiumshop.com, using iCat software. Launched in 1996, Stadium Shop is selling more than 30,000 sporting good items and is generating over 500,000 hits a month. The store cost between $25,000 and $30,000 to build, and broke even in the first year of operation.

■ CATALOG USER IMPLEMENTATION: UNDER ONE ROOF

Under One Roof is a nonprofit organization based in San Francisco that sells goods to benefit AIDS research and care. Located in the Castro district, the 1,000-square-foot store began looking for a way to expand both its retail and catalog operations to generate new revenue and broaden its reach beginning in the spring of 1996. Selling products such as jewelry, clothing, gourmet food, and pet care items, Under One Roof generates roughly $1 million a year, and all of its profits go to more than 50 agencies providing support to the AIDS community, such as the San Francisco Aids Community and Pets Are Wonderful Support.

"We wanted to take our retail and catalog business to the next step," said Beth Feingold, chief financial officer and treasurer for Under One Roof. The store thought the Internet would be the perfect way to expand its business and provide access to an audience beyond the San Francisco area.

Through a relationship with Miller/Shandwick, a Boston-based public relations firm that represents Intershop, Under One Roof developed an online storefront using Intershop Online, which Intershop donated to the nonprofit organization. In addition, Under One Roof received pro bono services from San Francisco-based CKS Media, which designed the storefront, and Ironlight Digital, a San Francisco Internet service provider which provided free hosting and maintenance services.

The project took roughly three months to implement, at an estimated cost of more than $100,000, all of which was donated. The bulk of the costs were in Web development from CKS, and other big items were Web hosting and connectivity, provided by Ironlight. The store has been busy promoting the site through listings on more than 90 search engine sites and some free advertising. However, business isn't great yet. "I had hoped it would kick us to a new level of business, but it hasn't happened yet," said Feingold. "I'm not making a million dollars off it."

However, adds Feingold, "I'm pragmatic enough to understand that we got into it early. We probably have another year before it makes the huge surge that everyone is hoping for," she said, pointing to issues such as consumer confidence in security and getting used to shopping in this new medium.

■ MICROSOFT COMMERCE: TARGETING BUSINESS-TO-BUSINESS

In April 1998, Microsoft Corp., in Redmond, Washington, released Microsoft Site Server 3.0 Commerce Edition, an Internet commerce server targeted at mid-size to large companies interested in building business-to-consumer and business-to-business electronic commerce sites. Site Server Commerce Edition counts among its customers: Office Depot, BarnesandNoble.com, 1-800-FLOWERS, Eddie Bauer, Tower Records, and other successful electronic commerce businesses. The software is priced starting at $4,609 per server, including 25 client access licenses, or $5,599 per server with 50 client access licenses.

"Doing business online is not just taking transactions over the Web," said Gytis Barzdukas, product manager of Internet commerce marketing at Microsoft, explaining Microsoft's electronic commerce strategy. "It is automating everything that businesses do in the physical world, from lead generation, market research and advertising to trading with business partners."

Microsoft Site Server 3.0 Commerce Edition includes the three following areas:

1. *Engage:* Helps businesses create commerce sites and applications, target online advertising and marketing, and personalize promotions. Features for the Engage module include:

➤ Ad Server, to host online advertisements.

➤ Intelligent CrossSell, to automate the running of promotions and cross-selling.

➤ Buy Now, a direct marketing tool that lets companies present product information and order forms, or capture customer profile information, within ad banners or other online formats.

➤ Site Server Personalization and Membership, which automatically generates Active Server Pages script.

➤ Database and Database Schema Independence.

➤ Site Foundation Wizard, which allows the server administrator to create a site's infrastructure, including its virtual directory and physical directories.

➤ Site Builder Wizard, which lets merchants create individual sites or stores, including stores with multi-level departments.

➤ Commerce Sample Sites—five ready-to-use templates—based on Active Server Pages that provide complete examples of working commerce applications.

➤ Integration with Microsoft Visual InterDev, an integrated development system for building dynamic Web applications.

➤ Content Deployment, which lets site administrators separate the development site from the actual production site.

➤ Pipeline Configuration Editor, an editing tool that allows the site manager to modify the Order Processing or Commerce Interchange pipelines.

➤ Commerce Server Software Development Kit (SDK), which helps sites create custom-order processing components.

➤ Microsoft Wallet Software Development Kit (SDK), tools for third parties to extend the Microsoft payment platform with their payment types.

➤ Migration and compatibility from Commerce Server 2.0 to Commerce Server.

2. *Transact:* Lets customers conduct financial transactions online, with secure and scalable order capture, management, and routing. Features include:

➤ Corporate Purchasing Support, including employee authentication, purchase order workflow and approval, a procurement catalog schema, and support for multiple purchase order output types.

➤ Commerce Interchange Pipeline, a system that allows for the interchange of structured business information using the Internet or existing EDI systems.

➤ Order Processing Pipeline, a series of stages for managing orders according to specific business rules.

➤ Windows NT Integration.

➤ Windows NT Security Support.

➤ Integration with Microsoft Internet Information Server 4.0.

➤ Integration with Microsoft Transaction Server.

➤ Microsoft Wallet Integration.

3. *Analyze:* Helps businesses understand customer and partner purchase and usage data, and factor in the changes to improve electronic commerce. Features include:

➤ Analysis, including in-depth site traffic and purchasing analysis.

➤ Purchase and order history, including the ability to store a customer's receipt.

➤ Site Server Administrator, providing a centralized management tool for all Site Server administrative functions.

➤ Promotion and Cross Sell Manager, to help marketing manager set up cross-sells and up-sells.

➤ Order Manager, which provides direct access to data on sales by month, year, product, shopper, and overall product sales.

"Web commerce is not a simple solution," said Barzdukas. "The complicated thing about it is, there is a lot of interaction with a lot of different parties and a lot of different technologies. You're talking about potentially thousands of relationships with different companies with different systems," he said, pointing to systems for product databases, payment processing, tax calculations, and customer profiles. "What we are trying to accomplish with Site Server is set the foundation to give businesses the basic functionality to conduct commerce on the Web and extend, integrate, and enhance as they need to."

Microsoft's solution is designed to be open and extendable to other systems that provide more sophisticated functions, such as payment processing by CyberCash or backend transaction processing by companies such as Open Market Inc. For a more thorough discussion of high-end commerce solutions, see Chapter 6. For payment processing options, see Chapter 7.

For information: Microsoft Corp., One Microsoft Way, Redmond, WA 98052-6399, (800) 426-9400, www.microsoft.com.

■ IBM E-BUSINESS

IBM's electronic commerce strategy is called e-business, and it includes hardware and software for security through transaction processing. For Web commerce, IBM offers Net.Commerce merchant server software for both business-to-consumer and business-to-business applications. Priced starting at $4,999, Net.Commerce is designed for businesses and merchants that want to run their own online shops or sell directly to business end users. In addition, if companies want to scale their Net.Commerce applications to multiple processors, IBM charges additional fees. Net.Commerce is the software on which other IBM electronic commerce solutions are based. "We're totally focused on upward scalability and backend integration," said Tom Patterson, chief strategist for electronic commerce at IBM.

IBM has gained several big-name clients with Net.Commerce, including Borders Books and Music, a $1 billion bookseller that is using the software to set up an online store; Aero-Marine Products, a $5 billion manufacturer which plans to put its catalog of 80,000 electronic components on the Web; and Hoffmaster, which manufactures disposable tableware.

Net.Commerce includes the following features:

➤ *SET support:* Incorporates the industry standard for Secure Electronic Transactions (SET), developed by a consortium headed up by MasterCard, Visa, IBM, Netscape, VeriSign, and others. For a more thorough discussion of SET, see Chapter 8.

➤ *Intelligent Catalog Technology:* Provides a "virtual sales assistant" for browsing catalogs and obtaining product information.

➤ *ODBC support:* Allows merchants to use the software with content contained in industry databases such as Oracle, Sybase, Informix, and others.

➤ *Support for Netscape Enterprise Web servers:* Lets companies extend existing Web sites running on Netscape servers to include electronic storefronts.

In addition, IBM has partnered with development companies such as Taxware International, First Virtual Holdings, and others to provide custom applications for tax calculation, payment processing, and other functions that IBM does not provide. The key strengths to Net.Commerce are its backend integration, allowing merchants to plug right into an Oracle, Informix or other database, frontend

intelligence that allows businesses to set up catalogs and provide streamlined searching capabilities for hundreds of
thousands of products, and SET compliance.

For information: IBM Corp., Internet Division, Route 100-
S01, Somers, NY 10589, (800) 365-4426, ext. 720, www.ibm.com.

Chapter 6 will look at higher end Web commerce solutions, for both business-to-consumer and business-to-business
operations.

Chapter

High-End Commerce Solutions

While lower cost merchant server and catalog software may be fine for businesses that want to sell products or services in a straightforward manner without a lot of customization, businesses that want more flexibility for product presentation, specialization in ordering and pricing, and more sophisticated integration with back-end systems are turning to commerce solutions that come with a higher price tag. Some of these solutions are geared more toward front-end presentation, such as Broadvision, which specializes in personalized marketing and dynamic page generation. Others, such as Connect and Actra, focus on targeted solutions such as business-to-business applications. Finally, high-end systems from companies such as Open Market and Interworld provide solutions for transaction processing and work-flow automation. This chapter will describe some of the commerce solutions that have been developed by these market leaders, and some user implementations. While some of these products compete, each of these solutions is targeted at specific segments of the Web commerce market. Businesses interested in pursuing these solutions should request bids, as they would for any other service, in order to fairly evaluate the offerings.

■ NETSCAPE COMMERCEXPERT

Actra was a joint venture of Netscape Communications Corp. and GE Information Services, based in Sunnyvale, California. Founded in 1996 to combine Netscape's expertise in developing and marketing Internet software and GEIS's experience in providing business-to-business electronic commerce solutions, Actra was acquired by Netscape in late 1997.

Netscape's family of electronic commerce products is called Netscape CommerceXpert, and it includes the following five products for buying, selling, and merchandising over the Internet:

> ➤ *Netscape ECXpert:* Provides Electronic Data Interchange (EDI) over the Internet through secure communications and standards-based, interoperable technology. ECXpert is the foundation product for Netscape's CommerceXpert family, and is the bridge to other products in this family. Priced starting at $75,000 for a two-CPU (central processing unit) license.

> ➤ *Netscape Xpert Seller:* Allows companies to set up online sales channels for corporate buyers, providing order management, seller and buyer maintained membership, payment options, electronic product catalogs, and EDI capability. Priced starting at $195,000 for a two-CPU license.

> ➤ *Netscape Xpert Buyer:* Complements Netscape Seller Xpert as an Internet procurement system in a multi-supplier, inter-enterprise environment. Priced starting at $250,000 for a two-CPU license.

> ➤ *Netscape Xpert Merchant:* The next release of Netscape Merchant System, based on Netscape Seller

ECXpert, that allows companies to set up online, personalized Internet storefronts with one-to-one dynamic content presentation.

➤ *Netscape Xpert Publishing:* The next release of Netscape Publishing System that provides a turnkey solution for companies that want to publish and sell online content and services. It features Web publishing, content and document management, customer service interfaces, search engines, a range of payment options and user agent technology for tracking and target marketing.

While Netscape offers solutions for business-to-consumer with the latter two products, its primary thrust is business-to-business, focusing on two key applications:

1. EDI over the Internet, with NetscapeXpert, and
2. Corporate purchasing over the Internet with Netscape BuyerXpert and SellerXpert.

➤ EDI Application

It is now estimated that roughly 80,000 companies are using EDI, which allows for secure electronic transfer of information, including funds for payment between buyers and sellers, over private data networks, also called value added networks (VANs). Companies that have implemented EDI utilize tools from software companies such as Sterling and Harbinger to transform and encrypt data and send it over closed, proprietary networks operated by companies such as GEIS and IBM Advantis. Now, with the advent of the Internet and open, platform-independent trading systems being developed, companies are looking at ways to integrate their existing EDI infrastructure with newer technologies. (See Chapter 9.)

The advantages of EDI over the Internet include lower implementation costs, open communications, and wider reach, with companies not having to be tied to specific vendors or networks. However, many companies that have invested heavily in EDI infrastructure do not want to scrap their investments and are concerned about how they'll integrate their existing systems with newer solutions, not to mention how these solutions will comply with standards for EDI still being developed by groups such as the Internet Engineering Task Force (IETF).

Netscape, through its relationship with GEIS, which manages business-to-business electronic trading for more than 40,000 trading partners, has developed ECXpert to address some of these issues.

"Every corporate customer wants to do things individually," said Ray Rike, former vice president of sales and marketing for Actra. "We need applications that focus outside of the enterprise." With this interenterprise approach in mind, Netscape has built some of the following features into ECXpert:

➤ Compliant with EDI Internet Integration (EDIINT), a work group of the IETF is developing standards for EDI over the Internet.

➤ S\MIME (secure e-mail standard) and SSL (secure data encryption).

➤ Connections to legacy EDI networks.

➤ Java user interfaces.

➤ Self-issue or third-party certificates for identification.

For more information on security and standards relating to electronic commerce, see Chapter 8. Netscape is targeting two primary markets with ECXpert:

1. Large corporations that either have mature EDI systems in place, such as those in the automotive and grocery industries.

2. Businesses that don't have mature EDI programs in place because they don't want to limit their trading partners to a proprietary system.

ECXpert, which runs in the Sun Solaris and Windows NT operating environments, allows companies to pass data directly from existing EDI systems into ECXpert and then on to trading partners. On the client side, ECXpert trading partners need to have a browser that supports FTP (file transfer protocol) and SMTP (e-mail) for data transfer, and one such as the Netscape Communicator that is compliant with EDI-INT standards for integrated EDI.

Some applications that utilize ECXpert include distributing sales information contained in an Excel spreadsheet over the Internet to integrate with SAP data forecasting, or transforming a purchase order into an HTML form and sending it to receiving systems. "Now you can leverage your Internet EDI infrastructure without requiring your customer to have EDI knowledge," said Rike.

The average implementation time for ECXpert is 30 to 60 days, and it's recommended that at least two people be dedicated to the implementation, including a database administrator or developer who understands EDI and Internet-based technology and a project coordinator or business manager who is designated to get business decisions made quickly.

➤ Corporate Purchasing over the Internet

With its SellerXpert and BuyerXpert products, Netscape is keying in on one of the hottest areas in Web commerce: Automating corporate buying and selling over the Internet with a standards-compliant, open system. While many businesses, such as Cisco Systems, have created successful Web-based marketplaces in which to sell their products and services directly to business customers and resale partners, and other businesses provide automated ordering systems over proprietary purchasing networks, a way for businesses to incorporate their existing buying and selling systems into an open model is still missing.

For example, as noted in Chapter 3, Cisco customer Cellular One liked the capabilities provided by CCO for buying products such as routers and switches, but it did not have a way to incorporate those online buying features into its existing procurement system that manages purchasing for more than 20 vendors. While Cisco is working on rolling out a solution that will link CCO directly to a corporation's intranet, other suppliers may not be as far along in this process. That's why Netscape (and other companies that will be discussed later in this chapter) has created its Seller and Buyer products. SellerXpert allows corporations to set up an online presence by creating a sophisticated product catalog and purchasing mechanism that has EDI integration capabilities. SellerXpert goes beyond catalog solutions provided by companies such as Microsoft and iCat by providing dynamic page generation, in which information is presented based on user profiles that are created on the buyer side (for example, one company may want to see a product catalog that contains only office furniture but no office supplies), and more importantly, it provides the EDI payment facilitation, which is a key component in business-to-business transactions. Since most companies don't buy with credit cards, providing secure payment processing over SSL or through relationships with vendors such as CyberCash are not enough for corporate purchasing. Companies need to have a way to allow their corporate buyers to identify which users are authorized to buy products, set up authorization and approval processes based on business logic, and create a mechanism for processing purchase orders over the Internet, as well as providing integration with existing EDI systems, if desired. SellerXpert provides these capabilities.

On the buyer side, companies need a way to efficiently automate the purchasing of products from multiple vendors. With BuyerXpert, businesses can set up a virtual catalog that includes products from all of their major vendors on the Internet, and automate the purchasing of these products, including integrating with existing EDI systems.

"The single largest issue is product catalog interoperability," said Rike. "When dealing with multiple suppliers, how do you ensure that your employee can identify products?" To provide interoperability among different suppliers, Netscape plans to support the Open Buying Interface (OBI) standards now being developed by a consortium headed up by American Express. It also plans to incorporate a rules-based engine and is now considering the Calico CAIT engine, to conduct searches on products that require complex configuration and variable pricing.

The average implementation time for both SellerXpert and BuyerXpert is five to six months. Netscape recommends three to five people on the project team, including at least one developer familiar with EDI and Internet-based technology and at least one business executive who has decision-making authority. During the implementation, approximately 25 to 30 percent of the project time includes mapping out the information flows that exist today, both internal and external to the organization; approximately 25 to 30 percent of the time includes defining legacy integration requirements and how the data structure exists today; about 40 percent is spend on the actual integration. For information: Netscape Communications Corp., 501 East Middle Field Rd., Mountain View, CA 94043, (650) 937-2600, www.netscape.com.

■ BROADVISION ONE-TO-ONE

Broadvision Inc., based in Redwood City, California, provides a software application system for developing end-to-end personalized electronic commerce sites. Broadvision's strength is in developing front-end, dynamic content presentation, although it also provides transaction processing through APIs that let companies integrate with existing payment, shipping, and handling systems.

Broadvision's personalized approach, through which marketers can target their Web site information to individual users based on customer profile information, is the driving force behind Broadvision's application system, called One-to-One. Broadvision One-to-One, priced starting at $60,000 with the average sale around $250,000, is targeted at Fortune 1000 companies and other organizations that want to build solutions for secure, personalized electronic commerce.

Founded in 1993, Broadvision specializes in commerce solutions for financial services, retail, travel, media, telecommunications, and other industries. Its customers include Kodak, US West, Liberty Financial, American Airlines, and more than 60 other clients who are using One-to-One in-house or to build solutions for their customers. One-to-One is used primarily in business-to-consumer applications, although Broadvision is now developing applications for the business-to-business environment. One-to-One lets businesses do the following:

➤ Tailor content to the preferences, requirements, and characteristics of individuals.

➤ Personalize content using a variety of matching techniques such as searches and community filtering.

➤ Establish communities of interest that link visitors together by matching their interests and behaviors with community-based Web site services and content.

Here are some examples of the types of things businesses can do with One-to-One:

1. Remind a visitor that her mother's birthday is coming up, and offer gift ideas and incentives such as coupons redeemable at an online flower shop.

2. Sell ad space to companies that target specific audience segments.

3. Add new content and eliminate outdated information without modifying application logic or HTML pages.

➤ Dynamic Command Center

The core feature of One-to-One is the Dynamic Command Center, through which marketing, advertising, and editorial managers define business rules that dictate changes in editorial content, ad placement, product pricing, or promotional incentives through a point-and-click interface. By defining business rules, marketing managers can implement strategies such as upselling or cross-selling, in which specific products or services are recommended based on past or current user buying behavior. For example, if a user purchased a CD from a particular band over a Web site, the site might greet the visitor with a message such as the following the next time he logged on: "Hey, Joe. We noticed that you bought a 'Smashing Pumpkins' CD last month. 'Smashing Pumpkins' has a new CD out, priced at $11.99. If you buy it today, we'll give you a 10 percent discount."

In a real application, Internet radio service NetRadio Network used One-to-One software to let users coming to its site create customized radio programming based on personal profiles. When users go to the NetRadio site, they enter their music preferences and other demographic information, and the site creates personalized play lists based on the information. NetRadio also links users to other sites based on their music preferences and recommends products and services from its online store.

The Dynamic Command Center is used to set up Web commerce sites, with an implementation period of roughly five months, based on a project team of both technical and business-side executives, while another Broadvision technology called Personal Sales Assistant manages the actual transaction process once the commerce sites are up and running. A description of the transaction flow using One-to-One is:

1. Visitor logs onto home page.
2. Views products.
3. Adds products to shopping cart.
4. Makes purchase.
5. Order is priced.
6. Order is created in database.
7. Payment is authorized.

8. Order is sent to external order fulfillment system.

9. Order is fulfilled by external order fulfillment system.

10. Payment is settled.

Broadvision One-to-One is suited for large businesses that may have thousands of products to sell, with variable pricing or configurations, and do not want to be limited to the static content presentations often associated with lower-cost electronic catalog solutions. One-to-One's higher price tag reflects a more sophisticated way of setting up and presenting content for electronic commerce sites, as well as back-end database integration often not available with lower-cost solutions. For information: Broadvision Inc., 585 Broadway, Redwood City, CA 94063, (800) 269-9375, www.broadvision.com.

■ CONNECT ONESERVER

Connect Inc., based in Mountain View, California, plays in the same space as Netscape and Broadvision, although it's been at it longer. Founded in 1987 as a spin-off of AppleLink messaging technology, Connect started out creating communications and messaging applications for virtual private networks. Connect rolled out its first Web-based software, called OneServer, in 1995, to provide an end-to-end solution for Internet commerce, including personalized and dynamically generated content on the front end and transaction processing on the back end, for both business-to-business and business-to-consumer applications. OneServer is priced starting at about $100,000 per processor.

Like Broadvision's One-to-One software, Connect's OneServer application encodes business rules to let Web sites target individual users and then build custom pages recommending specific products and services. However, while Broadvision has primarily targeted business-to-consumer applications, Connect is targeting business-to-business applications, enabling businesses to identify purchasing customers and then present tailored electronic catalogs or specific products, as well as incorporating terms that might include volume discounts or negotiated pricing.

Connect competes more directly with Netscape for business-to-business Web commerce customers. Like Netscape, Connect has developed specific applications to automate corporate selling and buying, although Connect's products have been on the street longer.

Connect offers the following vertically focused applications:

➤ OrderStream, launched in June 1996, which streamlines and automates the sales channel for business-to-business resellers and distributors. Priced starting at about $100,000 per processor.

➤ PurchaseStream, launched in May 1997, which is the buy-side complement to OrderStream, providing a Web-based purchasing system for indirect goods and services. Priced starting at about $100,000 per processor.

➤ OrderStream

OrderStream is built on the OneServer application platform, but instead of working with custom-coded business logic, OrderStream uses a set of prepackaged business objects to deliver a vertically focused application. OrderStream supports resellers and distributors of various products, including computers, software, and office supplies, which are usually sold under volume contracts through published catalogs.

With OrderStream, employees can use their Web browser to search a distributor's or reseller's online catalog, dynamically building purchase orders from a desktop computer. Catalogs can be configured on a per-employee basis to show only those products a given department is allowed to buy. Employees authorized to buy products can look at pricing specific to a contract and check inventory in real time.

Orders that need approval are forwarded to the appropriate person, then move to the reseller's or distributor's order fulfillment system.

Connect is targeting three areas within a purchasing corporation with OrderStream:

1. The purchasing department, for purchasing controls.
2. The buyer or requisitioner, for electronic order, creation, submission, and order tracking.
3. The approver, for order approval or rejection.

On the reseller and distributor end, OrderStream supports the following functions:

1. The customer service representative, for customer inquiry and service.
2. The catalog manager, for catalog presentation and branding.
3. The product manager, for product database management.
4. The system administrator, for system administration.

The benefits to using OrderStream include increasing revenues for resellers and distributors and cutting costs for end users, says Connect. "We want to mimic the contractual relationship that exists between buyer and seller," said Pam Kostka, director of product marketing for Connect. Some of those terms and conditions might include customer-specific pricing or delivery terms based on prior ordering history. OrderStream customers include Compaq Computer Corp., Comark, Moore Kensington Daytimers, and others.

The implementation period for OrderStream is anywhere from two weeks to six months, although Connect also offers a QuickStart application that can be up and running within 30 days, for $130,000 to $150,000 including licensing and services. For OrderStream implementation, Connect recommends having an Oracle database administrator, an

HTML programmer, and at least one business side person who can define the business logic and manage content.

OrderStream is based on an Oracle 7 database and utilizes a Fulcrum text search engine, including RSA encryption. Core to the architecture is an object layer that is wrapped around the core technologies, which simplifies working with the underlying technologies and provides a more robust environment. It runs in the Sun, Unix, and NT environments. In addition to providing dynamic content presentation, order capture, and order management, OrderStream also provides financial transaction processing and integration with existing Enterprise Resource Package (ERP) systems such as those provided by SAP and PeopleSoft.

➤ PurchaseStream

In May 1997, Connect introduced PurchaseStream, the buy-side complement to OrderStream that automates corporate purchasing from users' desktops. While OrderStream is targeted at resellers and distributors, PurchaseStream is targeted at large corporations, typically $1 billion and up, that spend upwards of $500 million a year on office furniture, computers, janitorial supplies, and other indirect goods.

According to purchasing industry estimates, companies spend an average of between $100 and $150 per order on costs associated with processing the order, specifically human resource costs. With PurchaseStream, companies can significantly cut these costs and let their purchasing employees spend time on more valuable functions such as establishing relationships and negotiating deals with vendors.

PurchaseStream automates the purchasing cycle of acquiring indirect goods, from product purchase through invoice and payment, including the following capabilities:

➤ Personalized electronic catalogs.

➤ Contract pricing.

➤ Product availability.

➤ Product selection and comparison.

➤ Purchase controls.

➤ Approval routing.

➤ Order submission.

➤ Electronic payment.

➤ Online order tracking.

➤ Buyer purchasing and exception reporting.

➤ Seller performance reporting.

With PurchaseStream, employees use standard Web browsers to access a vendor mall of approved suppliers and order products from custom electronic catalogs based on their needs and authorization limits. Orders that fall within established purchasing limits are sent directly to the supplier for fulfillment, while those that don't are routed electronically for approval. Online payment options include blanket purchase orders, electronic purchase orders, and electronic procurement cards, which are the credit cards of the business-to-business world. The average time to get PurchaseStream up and running is about the same as for OrderStream, with the same type of human resource requirements. Connect also offers a QuickStart version of PurchaseStream, which takes about 30 days to install.

Like OneServer and OrderStream, PurchaseStream is based on open standards including Unix and Oracle 7, utilizes a Fulcrum text search engine and is protected with security from RSA Data Security, VeriSign, and SSL. For more information on security, see Chapter 8. For information: Connect Inc., 515 Ellis St., Mountain View, CA 94043-2242, (800) 262-2638, www.connectinc.com.

■ OPEN MARKET

Open Market, based in Cambridge, Massachusetts, has been developing high-end solutions for Internet commerce since its founding in April 1994. Known primarily as a provider of heavy-duty transaction processing systems for electronic commerce, Open Market started out as a consulting and custom-job company and counted among its first clients Time Warner Inc.'s Pathfinder site and Advance Publications. While Open Market's core competency is in developing and delivering solutions for backend processing and management, the company has been forging alliances recently to provide more frontend commerce capabilities, such as partnering with iCat Corp. to help companies create Web catalogs, and acquiring Waypoint Software Corp., which develops business-to-business electronic catalogs.

Open Market is targeting the following types of businesses with its commerce solutions:

1. Large corporations, such as Walt Disney, Time Warner, and C/Net, that want to own the infrastructure and have the information system resources in-house to operate high-end Web commerce operations.

2. Commerce service providers, such as AT&T and MCI, that use Open Market software to develop solutions for their customers.

3. Business-to-business manufacturers and distributors, such as AMP, that want to establish online catalogs.

4. Business publishers, such as Lexis/Nexis and Simba, that want to establish new channels for providing high-end information to business professionals.

Open Market's strategy is to separate content management from transaction management, which means that it centrally locates its transaction management software on servers that typically reside at the client's site, and interfaces with content that can be located on its customers' servers anywhere in the world. Open Market's customers typically have an existing Web site, and are looking for high-volume transaction processing capabilities.

Open Market's primary software products include:

➤ *OM-Transact:* Provides complete back-office infrastructure for secure Internet commerce. Priced starting at $250,000.

➤ *SecureLink:* Enables a business to offer goods and services for sale on the Web.

➤ *OM-Axcess:* Centrally manages business transactions using data distributed across the Web.

➤ *Magellan:* Helps companies build business-to-business catalogs on the Internet.

Additionally, Open Market offers the following products:

➤ *Secure WebServer:* Web server software on which secure Web sites can be built. Priced at $895 for one processor and $360 for each additional processor.

➤ *WebReporter:* Lets companies analyze their Web site's server activity. Priced at $495 for one processor and $195 for each additional processor.

➤ *ActiveCommerce DB:* Allows companies to create dynamic, commerce-enabled business Web sites.

Open Market sees its primary competition coming not from other high-end commerce providers such as Netscape, Connect, and Broadvision, nor from solutions providers such as IBM or Microsoft, whose software and services are targeted at companies large or small, but from "companies that think they can do this stuff themselves," said Wendy Ziner, director of marketing communications at Open Market. That would include large companies with significant IT resources that write their own code, usually with C programming and utilizing HTML for Web documents, to create Web commerce enabled sites.

Open Market believes it brings an end-to-end perspective to electronic commerce, with OM-Transact being at the core of its solutions.

➤ OM-Transact

OM-Transact was introduced in March 1996 as a back-office system to handle electronic ordering, payment, and billing for business-to-consumer Web commerce applications. In December 1996, Open Market introduced new features that support business-to-business commerce, including API links to order and entry fulfillment systems, EDI, and enterprise systems. OM-Transact's architecture, which separates content management from transaction processing, supports multiple content servers, meaning that when thousands of buyers are reviewing and ordering products from different servers, each transaction is conducted by a single processing system.

The benefits to this type of architecture include scalability, flexibility, and increased security. For example, Time Warner Inc. uses OM-Transact to manage transactions on its high-volume Pathfinder site and to interface with customer account information residing on company databases. Bruce Judson, former general manager of Time Inc. New Media in New York, said, "By maintaining account information in a separate area, the security of the entire system is dramatically enhanced, as opposed to having account information distributed with the content."

OM-Transact provides:

➤ Security through SSL encryption.

➤ Authentication through access control for a registered set of customers.

➤ Online account creation.

➤ One-to-one marketing through a user-profile API that supports customized content and pricing.

➤ Web page editor for screen layout customization.

➤ Order management, including order acceptance, shopping cart support, tax and shipping charge calculation, fulfillment notification, and electronic software downloads.

➤ Secure payment processing through credit cards, CyberCash, and SET.

➤ Online authorization and settlement.

➤ Purchase order support for account-based purchases.

➤ Flexible subscriptions with trials, grace periods, pay-per-view, and credits.

➤ Online customer service.

➤ Record keeping, such as online, real-time transaction records for merchants, order reports, and transaction activity audit trail.

➤ Back-office systems integration, including EDI and ERP systems.

➤ Additional Products

Open Market offers additional software that works with OM-Transact. SecureLink is designed for companies that do not yet have commerce-enabled Web sites, providing the technology that lets them embed digital offers into their Web content so they can sell hard goods, soft goods, and subscriptions in an online store. OM-Axcess is software that centrally manages end-user authentication and authorization to distributed Web applications, aimed at corporate intranet users.

Magellan is one of Open Market's newest products, introduced in late 1997, which helps industrial catalog publishers create an online channel. Magellan uses a database to house product information and graphics, and automatically generates custom part numbers, configurations, and prices. Magellan also helps industrial Web site builders dynamically generate technical specification detail pages using templates and data from the product database, or link to pages maintained on any Web site. It also includes catalog management, which lets companies update the catalog onsite or remotely, using Magellan's browser-based authoring tool. For information: Open Market Inc., 245 First St.,

Cambridge, MA 02142, (888) OPEN-MKT or (617) 949-7000, www.openmarket.com.

■ INTERWORLD

InterWorld Technology Ventures specializes in business-to-consumer and business-to-business integrated solutions. Founded in 1994, InterWorld is a New York-based, privately held corporation that's backed by Microsoft co-founder Paul Allen, investment banking firm Donaldson, Lufkin & Jenrette, and other investors.

InterWorld is one of the few Internet commerce software companies not based in Silicon Valley, and its geographic location provides some interesting perspective on the company's philosophy.

"The most complex, object-oriented systems are on Wall Street," said Michael Donahue, president and chief technology officer at InterWorld, pointing to the sophisticated financial information systems built and maintained by the big banking firms in New York. "Therefore, most of the object-oriented programmers with expertise building mission critical, scalable, secure transaction processing systems are here," adds Donahue.

InterWorld's key strength is its open, scalable architecture that allows companies to plug in just about any component. That's because the system in based on object-oriented technology, utilizing APIs that companies can write to if objects, or components, in the electronic commerce system change, whether that's a single product price or an operating system.

InterWorld rolled out early versions of its software beginning in 1995, although it didn't have a commercial rollout until March 1997. InterWorld's core product is called Commerce Exchange, priced starting at $75,000, although the average deal price is $150,000. Commerce Exchange is an end-to-end solution for electronic commerce that's based on what InterWorld calls a "Four Pillar approach," providing:

1. Architecture.
2. Tools.
3. Transaction processing.
4. Applications.

➤ Architecture

Commerce Exchange utilizes InterWorld's Object Architecture and Scalable Operating System (Oasis), a high-performance, scalable architecture that provides a backbone into which application modules can be plugged. The Oasis technology allows legacy data from mainframes, flat files, and relational data sources to be integrated into the object-oriented framework. Also included in the InterWorld architecture is a search engine, distributed transaction management system, and dynamic load balancing. "The enterprise is made up of a lot of operating systems, database servers, and applications," said Donahue. "Our architecture fits into whatever you have in the enterprise. Like Java, it runs on anything."

That's important for businesses that require a high degree of customization with their Web commerce operations, and need to integrate their transaction processing system into existing systems such as inventory management, order fulfillment, accounts payable, and other systems. With Commerce Exchange, InterWorld is targeting Fortune 1000 companies that expect to generate a high volume of transactions in the hundreds of millions of dollars with either business-to-consumer or business-to-business Web sites, and that need to have an open and flexible architecture that can scale and change as business grows.

The average implementation time for Commerce Exchange is three months for systems requiring full database integration, with between 6 and 12 people dedicated to the project, including both IS and business executives. Oasis is bundled with Commerce Exchange, but for a stand-alone custom development solution it is priced beginning at $10,000.

➤ Tools

Commerce Exchange also comes with Oasis Workplace, which is a set of visual tools for developers and managers to use to build and manage applications. Oasis Workplace includes:

- ➤ Real-time, remote administration of all system components from any Web browser.
- ➤ Customer service administration for assignment of user and group profiles and privileges.
- ➤ Content administration and authoring.
- ➤ Management of merchant specific policies and business rules.
- ➤ Reporting.

➤ Transaction Processing

InterWorld Financial Exchange is the transaction processing engine component of Commerce Exchange, supporting business-to-consumer and business-to-business work flows. Financial Exchange automates the entire sales cycle, including:

- ➤ Security, through SSL, MD5, and RC4 data encryption standards.
- ➤ Scalable transaction processing.
- ➤ Multiple personal shopping baskets.
- ➤ Online subscriptions.
- ➤ Flexible order processing.
- ➤ Multiple payment processing options, including credit cards, purchase orders, or online accounts.
- ➤ Reseller and virtual mall environments.
- ➤ Web-based administration.

➤ Interfaces to legacy financial systems and third-party packages.

InterWorld Financial Exchange is workflow based and allows for seamless integration into other financial systems. For example, it provides an open API and full gateway into the LitleNet credit card processing network, and supports CyberCash and First Virtual payment systems.

➤ Applications

Commerce Exchange comes with an integrated suite of applications, including:

➤ InterWorld Catalog, which lets companies set up on-line catalogs with search capabilities, dynamic page generation and intuitive GUI-based (graphical user interface) administration; priced starting at $20,000 for one processor.

➤ InterWorld Customer Service, a secure, high-volume chat solution and Internet bulletin board solution with built-in private forums for help desk and customer service; priced starting at $20,000.

➤ InterWorld Digital Distribution, which provides secure distribution of digital goods such as software and content; priced starting at $30,000.

➤ InterWorld Auction, which allows companies to build dynamic online auctions for purposes of liquidating inventory; priced starting at $30,000.

InterWorld clients include Digital Equipment Corp., Broderbund Software, Platinum Software, Micro Warehouse, Multiple Zones International, Comdisco, Cliggott Publishing, and other companies. For information: InterWorld Technology Ventures Inc., 395 Hudson St., 6th floor, New York, NY 10014-3669, (800) 814-8942, ext. 35, www.interworld.com.

Payment Options: Getting the Money

Show me the money. That's really what it's all about, isn't it? You might be a one-person shop running your Web site out of a garage or a cybercafe, or a multibillion-dollar corporation investing millions in your electronic commerce systems. You might have complex, dynamically generated custom Web pages integrated with back-end databases, or simple catalogs on a single home page running on someone else's server. Regardless of the setup, the bottom line for Web commerce is having a way for the user to hit that buy button and make a payment.

In the real world, there are three ways of paying for goods: You can pay in cash, you can write a check, or you can use a credit card. The same mechanisms are becoming available to online merchants. You can take a credit card number, encrypt (or encode) it as it's transmitted, and process the order manually. You can take a credit card order and process it electronically. You can take a debit card number and process it like a credit card, although the buyer will treat it as a check. Or, you can take cash.

We'll discuss each of these options, starting with the one that's easiest to implement online, the credit card.

■ CREDIT CARDS

Credit cards have been processed electronically for decades. They started in restaurants and hotels, then went into stores, and their use was touted on television ads ("operators are standing by") as long as 20 years ago. A huge industry exists to process credit card transactions online, with companies like First Data Corp., Total Systems Corp., and National Data Corp. handling the back-office details for banks, their merchants, and credit card holders. Millions of stores around the nation feature terminals (Hewlett-Packard's Verifone unit is the leading manufacturer) through which cards are swiped, numbers are entered, and receipts are printed. Signing the receipt in person proves your identity, and the purchase.

Before you take credit cards over the Internet, you'll need a merchant identification. If you already have a business, you probably got one from your bank when you opened the doors. If you don't have one, you can get one quickly—the best way to start that process is to call your banker or visit a Web site which has the required form (e.g., Mercantec).

Using credit cards online today, however, is more like using them with an "operator standing by." The card number and transaction details are stored and processed, but there is no identification of the buyer, as there is when a payment slip is signed in a store. For this reason, credit card processors charge online merchants just as much to process a transaction as they charge a telephone merchant—usually about 50 cents. (Transactions handled through a terminal, by contrast, cost just 3 to 5 cents.)

On top of that fee is a discount applied by Visa and MasterCard, which are consortiums of banks, or American Express Co. and Discover, which are separate companies, for handling transactions. This means you'll pay 2 to 3 cents on the dollar taking Visa or MasterCard, slightly less for

Discover, and about 5 cents on the dollar with American Express. Credit agreements between the card companies and merchants prevent these costs from being passed on to customers. Discounts may also differ between users of the terminals, where a card is physically present, and a "card not present" environment like that found on a Web site. In exchange for the discounts, merchants are assured payment. Customers also get protection on returns, and limited protection against fraud or lost cards. (Credit insurance, sold by the banks that issue credit cards, covers the balance of this risk.)

What software does your Web store need to take credit cards? At a minimum, you should have some form of encryption, usually the Secure Sockets Layer (SSL) which is standard on Netscape and Microsoft browsers, which means your server will need an encryption key. Next, you'll need a shopping cart program that lets users collect items for purchase, calculate the costs and taxes, and deliver a finished bill for approval. Finally, if you don't want to enter your transaction files manually or as a single file or batch for processing, you need a transaction engine.

➤ Digital IDs

Server encryption keys, also known as digital IDs, are available through a number of certificate authorities, which authorize and maintain records on them. The largest certificate authority is run by VeriSign Inc., a company founded in 1995 specifically to handle digital certificates. The company handles digital ID requests for companies such as America Online, Microsoft, and Netscape, but you can file for a digital ID directly off the company's Web site. As of summer 1998, VeriSign was charging $349 for the first server ID a company purchased, and $249 for each additional ID. A 128-bit Global Server ID costs $695.

The underlying technology for VeriSign's digital ID is Secure Sockets Layer (SSL), originally created by RSA Technologies Inc., which is now a unit of Security Dynamics. Each message is encrypted with two codes, or keys, a string of bits that changes the digital values of data entering or leaving a program. The public key is used to scramble, or encrypt the message, while a second private key decrypts it. The private keyholders' identities are maintained by privately run certificate authorities, like VeriSign. A server digital ID allows you to digitally sign documents and prove your identity to a certificate authority.

➤ Shopping Carts

Mercantec's SoftCart Version 3.0 is typical of the online shopping cart programs now available. Once such software is installed on your Web server, you only need to add an HTML link from pages describing items to the page on which the shopping form will be located, plus a button for submitting the completed form to the processing engine, in order to do business. If your inventory is in the form of a database, you'll need the skills to write database calls to either a .dll (Windows) or .so (Unix) file.

Generally, the software will:

- ➤ Link purchase requests to a form.
- ➤ Complete the form, adding credit card information.
- ➤ Process the form, usually by writing the data in it to a file for batch processing (a separate program is needed for online transaction processing).
- ➤ E-mail a complete receipt to the customer verifying the transaction.
- ➤ Supply flexible order routing, so goods can be delivered and the order can be handled by your accounting department, or any other decision makers who need fast access to sales data.

Some programs also provide the following enhancements:

- ➤ Built-in searches of a product database.
- ➤ Support for Dynamic HTML objects, which could include prices that change quickly or are based on purchase quantities.

➤ Support for additional forms, like customer surveys or mailing lists, which shoppers complete using their e-mail clients.

➤ Electronic Data Interchange (EDI) support, for processing electronic purchase orders in a business-to-business environment.

This will be done within a secure (SSL) environment. The shopping cart software is linked to your SSL encryption key so all data transfers between your server and the client's browser (assuming it supports SSL) are encrypted and safe from interception.

➤ Transaction Processors

ICVerify, which merged with CyberCash in May 1998, is part of the new wave in Internet commerce. It's a transaction processor, a product which does all the work of an in-store terminal, except it does it on a Web site. ICVerify is available under Windows NT, in various versions of Unix, or as an Oracle database cartridge. Some knowledge of perl scripting is necessary to implement the software, but the company is building a network of integration partners to handle the workload.

ICVerify's software does what a merchant's terminal would do. It takes a user's credit card number, the merchant's identification number, and the transaction data (date, time, amount), formats it for your credit card processor, initiates the call, and completes the transaction. It also saves the settlement information and authorization code, which is a string of numbers printed on charge slips identifying each transaction completed by the processor. (The software can also handle batch processing, collecting data and processing it together at night.) The transaction data can then be run directly through your shopping cart software for processing of the order and for accounting.

The ICVerify package can be set up to handle multiple merchants, and it can process recurring transactions, as with credit sales and layaways. The module that handles the actual processing requires only 3.5 kilobytes of memory. The software also comes with modules for specific industries, and for handling corporate cards and discounts.

The biggest risk in taking credit cards by phone or on the Web (which leads to higher discounts for such transactions) is that the buyer may be using a stolen credit card or credit card number. ICVerify is among the products that can help protect against this kind of fraud by matching an address given by the buyer against databases of addresses maintained by credit card processing computers.

➤ CyberCash

CyberCash is best known as a transaction processing company. Based in Reston, Virginia, CyberCash provides a system called CashRegister that lets merchants offer their customers the following types of payment options:

1. Credit card payments, including Visa, MasterCard, American Express, or Discover.
2. CyberCoin, which lets users make purchases from 25 cents to $10.
3. Electronic checks, which provide check processing over the Internet.

CashRegister can be integrated into existing Web sites, and it currently works with Microsoft Windows NT and Unix-based Web servers. Merchants can implement the software on their own by downloading it from the CyberCash site (www.cybercash.com) for free, or by working with a mall operator, hosting service, or other Internet service provider that has an agreement to use CashRegister. While the CashRegister software is free, merchants compensate CyberCash by paying a few cents per transaction.

CashRegister is the software that runs on the business or merchant side. To use the system, consumers can either enter their credit card numbers into a Web form without any special software except a Web browser, or they can download free CyberCash Wallet software that lets them set up an account with credit card information, CyberCoins, and electronic checks. CyberCash offers several different payment systems that will be discussed next.

Credit Card Payments

The CyberCash Secure Internet Credit Card Service, which is part of CashRegister, was first introduced in April 1995. It lets consumers with a credit card buy products or services from merchants that have set up a CyberCash CashRegister. To implement the software, merchants need to download the merchant connection kit from the CyberCash Web site. Installing the software requires some knowledge of perl and HTML coding; details are in the download instructions.

Installation will integrate your site with CyberCash's server for payment processing.

Once the CashRegister software is implemented, merchants also need to set up an account with a bank to accept CyberCash credit card payments. The following North American banks support CyberCash:

➤ CheckFree Corp.
➤ First Data Corp.
➤ Global Payment Systems.
➤ NOVA Information System.
➤ Vital Processing Servers.

CyberCash replicates the same process of credit card processing over the Internet as is done in the real world. Here's how the typical credit card transaction process works:

1. Customer gives credit card to merchant.
2. Merchant, or sometimes the customer, swipes the card through a card reader.
3. Information in the magnetic strip of the card is transmitted to a credit card processor for authorization.

4. The credit card information is compared against a set of rules predefined by the credit card issuer (Visa, for example) for the customers, such as credit limit and expiration date.

5. Authorization is granted and sent back to the merchant as an authorization code.

6. Merchants put the authorization code on the charge slip.

CyberCash has automated this process through its software and through relationships with banks and credit card authorization networks. Once the Web customer's credit card number is entered into the CashRegister software, through the CyberCash Wallet or just by entering it into a form, CashRegister formats the transaction and sends it over the Internet to the processor for authorization. Once authorization is given, the response is sent back to the CashRegister software, where it confirms the purchase for the user. The process takes about 15 seconds. CashRegister runs on Solaris, SUNOS, SGI, HP-UX, BSDI, Windows, Linux, and Macintosh.

Internet Wallet

While customers shopping at CyberCash storefronts do not have to have any special software to buy products, with the exception of their Web browser through which they'd enter a credit card number into a form on a screen, they can set up an electronic wallet that gives them different payment options. The CyberCash Internet Wallet is set up on the customer's computer, and it provides the same payment options that CashRegister does, including:

1. Credit card payments.
2. CyberCoin payments.
3. Electronic checks.

To get Internet Wallet software, customers can go to www.cybercash.com and download it for free. Many Cyber-Cash merchants also give customers the ability to download the software right from their site, and CyberCash will help them figure out how to do that.

In setting up the software, customers establish a Wallet ID, which is a secure way of identifying them to merchants, much like a PIN number on your debit card. Also, merchants have an ID that identifies them to customers. For more information on security issues such as digital IDs and authentication on the Internet, see Chapter 8.

When setting up their Wallets, customers download the CyberCoin portion by withdrawing money from bank accounts, just like they'd do at an ATM. For the credit card portion, they can transfer amounts from their credit card account, which is processed like a regular transaction and not a cash advance, which typically involves fees. Then, once their Wallet is ready, customers can shop at storefronts that accept CyberCash payments.

CyberCoin is for micropayments, or small payments ranging from 25 cents to $10. Many products and services for sale on the Web, such as news articles or digital photographs, are priced in increments so low that customers don't want to use their credit cards, particularly if they have to pay a finance charge. For more expensive purchases, Wallet users might want to use their credit cards rather than CyberCoin. What's different about Wallet shoppers and non-Wallet shoppers who just enter a credit card number into the browser is that Wallet shoppers have an ID, so they can be authorized to the merchant, and an account set up with CyberCash to facilitate the payment process and provide additional benefits to the user. For example, the Wallet software and CashRegister software maintain a record of the transaction that appears on the next credit card statement.

For further information: CyberCash Inc., 2100 Reston Pkwy., Suite 430, Reston, Virginia 22091, (703) 620-4200, www.cybercash.com.

■ DIGICASH

DigiCash, based in Amsterdam, is a secure electronic payment company that pioneered ecash, electronic cash for use
over the Internet. Based on public key cryptography technology that allows users and banks to exchange digital signatures to verify each other's identity, ecash allows customers
to download digital money from bank accounts onto their
PCs to make electronic purchases.

DigiCash describes ecash as "like using a virtual ATM."
When users connect over the Internet to banks participating
in the ecash program, offering digital signatures for verifica-
tion, they can then withdraw digital coins stored on the hard
drive of their computer. Once they wish to make a purchase
from merchants linked to the ecash program, they transfer
these virtual "coins" from their PC browser to the merchant
server.

The client software, called a *purse,* has its own graphical
interface and works under Windows 3.1 and later. Merchants
participating in the program also need software provided by
DigiCash, which could range from a simple acceptance program to a comprehensive accounting system which includes
such functions as inventory control.

Ecash licensees include Deutsche Bank, Germany; Bank
Austria, Austria; Den Norske Bank, Norway; Advance Bank,
Australia; Nomura Research Institute, Japan; Mark Twain
Bank, USA; and Eunet, Finland. For more information,
visit www.digicash.com/ecash/ecash-issuers.html.

■ DIGITAL EQUIPMENT'S MILLICENT

Millicent is a microtransaction technology announced by
Digital Equipment Corp. in 1997. The system can handle
transactions worth as little as one-tenth of a cent. It's a system of protocols employing "brokers" for accumulating small
transactions into amounts large enough to be processed, and

a form of "scrip" (think of it as Web Green Stamps), which consists of a signed message stating that a particular message holds a particular value. The brokers are authorized to buy scrip from merchants at a discount, which makes all this worth their while.

Since the scrip has economic value only to its creator, it doesn't need the security required in a standard transaction. The vendors who issue such scrip, however, protect it by using encryption keys in the digests of their messages.

Digital Equipment Corp. president Robert Palmer describes Millicent scrip as the perfect vehicle for pay-per-use videogames, small text files like magazine articles, or individual stock quotes. Millicent launched in early 1998.

■ CHECKS

There are two ways in which your site can take checks. You can create virtual checks, or take payments using debit cards that link to checking accounts.

Debit cards look just like credit cards, except they directly access users' checking accounts. They're the descendants of the ATM cards that became popular in the early 1980s for withdrawing money from bank machines, and they're often still used in that way.

What has changed is that their transactions are now regularly processed through bank credit card networks. Most now carry logos for either Visa or MasterCard. What this means is you can process debit card transactions just like you would credit card transactions, but since the money is coming directly from users' checking accounts, discounts are lower.

➤ Redi-Check

Redi-Check Inc., Salt Lake City, Utah, a transaction processing company, announced an Internet Transaction Gateway it said would allow Internet merchants to accept checks online.

Redi-Check had been offering check guarantee services since its founding, and extended them to the Internet in March, 1997. Merchants can get processing, protection, or guarantees on checks which are created online.

To offer these services, Redi-Check uses the ABA numbers that are printed on paper checks, in the lower-left corner of the check. These numbers identify printed checks within the Federal Reserve system, identifying the bank and the customer. When a customer writes a check on a merchant's server, these numbers are passed directly to Redi-Check's server, then checked against the list of valid codes maintained by the Federal Reserve. Redi-Check can then handle the transaction processing as it would a debit card. Once that's done, both the customer and the merchant receive e-mails verifying the transaction.

There are three levels of protection offered by Redi-Check. In processing, the banks' number only is checked through a Federal Reserve database of financial institutions. In protection, the system used by many merchants that takes checks, the customer's checking account number is matched against a list of accounts with problems, like bad checks and closed accounts. A guaranteed check, as the name implies, guarantees the merchant will be paid, and allows them to immediately ship the product. Each level of service requires more processing and costs more money.

Not only does the Redi-Check system cost less for a merchant to operate, since it isn't subject to the discounts of credit cards, but it's also easy to implement, with only a few HTML codes required on your Web server pages, linking your order forms to Redi-Cash's server.

In 1998, Redi-Check was charging merchants a $249 up-front license fee, and a discount of 2 percent on all transactions, with a minimum check amount of $25. Check Protection requires another $15 set-up fee, plus a discount of .02 to .18 percent, depending on the size of the check. Check guarantee services are priced like insurance, carrying an additional $50 set-up fee and an additional discount of 1.5 percent for the first $500 of a transaction, 1.5 percent of the additional amount between $500 and $2,500, and a maximum $2,500 per check. Protection and guarantee services, however, are used independently of each other.

Most of the major Web commerce software, including catalog software from companies mentioned in Chapter 5, as well as higher end software such as that discussed in Chapter 6, and even most Internet service providers, mentioned in Chapter 4, support some combination of payment options. For further information on which payment options are offered or supported by software companies, contact the companies or the payment providers. The next chapter will discuss one of the hottest issues in Web commerce: Security.

Chapter 8

The Security Debate: Is the Web Safe for Commerce?

Is the Web safe? Yes, but if you're doing business on the Web, that's the wrong question to ask. The right questions are these:

What is encryption and how do you use it?

How do you convince customers your Web site is safe?

How do you secure your business operations from the rest of the Web?

How can you use security software to actually improve the way you do business?

The following discussion addresses these questions and offers possible solutions.

■ HOW DOES ENCRYPTION WORK?

All Internet security is based on the idea of encryption, coding messages so they look like garbage. Such codes have been a feature of military intelligence for centuries. Confederate and Union spies used codes, or ciphers, to send messages to their bosses. Both sides used encryption extensively during World War II. Victory over Nazi Germany was achieved, in part, by decoding many of Germany's messages.

If you've seen one of the "Little Orphan Annie Decoder Rings" Ovaltine issued in the 1930s, you know how these things work. A ring of numbers from 1–26 was moved against a ring containing the alphabet. The key might be as simple as D-13, meaning the letter D was equal to the number 13. Numbers would be read over the radio and kids would write them down, then set the decryption key with their rings and decode the message, which usually said something like "Drink More Ovaltine."

Modern encryption keys work similarly, except the keys are more complex. You can break the Orphan Annie Code by testing the message against the 26 numbers on the ring, to find a coherent message. But what if you had to match a hidden code of 40 random numbers, each of which operated on the message differently, before you could decode the message? What if you had to guess 150 numbers correctly, in the right order, before you had the key that would decrypt Annie's message.

That's how encryption keys work, but there's one more step. Two separate encryption keys are used. The first key scrambles the message so it can't be read, but the scrambling key may be readily available, or public. But decoding messages requires a second private key, held only by the person who created the message, or its intended recipient. In practice, the keys are related at their base, or root. That's why one key can unlock a second key's message.

To work, public-private key encryption needs someone to hold the private keys, in case they're lost, and in case the identity of the sender or recipient is questioned. The same company that hands out these private keys will maintain (and protect) them, acting as a certificate authority for private key encryption.

■ DIGITAL CERTIFICATES

Not all private keys or digital certificates are created equal. The simplest kind of digital certificate, called a Class 1 certificate, is easily obtainable by any consumer who visits the VeriSign Web site (www.verisign.com). All you need to do is give your name, address, and an e-mail address, and once your e-mail address is verified, you'll get a certificate. Think of it as a library card.

A Class 2 certificate requires proof of your physical address as well. For that, the company giving out the certificate will consult a credit database—Equifax or Experian in the case of consumers, Dun & Bradstreet in the case of businesses. This is more like a credit card.

The strongest type of digital certificate is called a Class 3 certificate. Think of this as a kind of driver's license. To get it you need to prove exactly who you are and prove you're responsible. Real driver's licenses have photos and printed or holographic technologies that keep them from being tampered with. Class 3 certificates are not being offered now, but companies involved in the security business do envision them being used in the future for things like apartment leases negotiated over the Web or loans acquired online. They could also be used as legal identifications, supporting the release of credit records or the delivery of court documents.

In today's form of electronic commerce, most individuals are getting Class 1 certificates, but some stores are getting Class 2 certificates, and consumers will start getting them once a technology called SET is available. (See the discussion of SET, on p. 124.)

■ SECURE SOCKETS LAYER

In theory, many companies can act as certificate authorities. VeriSign Inc. (www.verisign.com), Mountain View, California, is the leading certificate authority in the United

States. It, in turn, licenses the technology it uses from RSA Inc. (www.rsa.com). RSA holds patents on the public-private key technology introduced in 1976 by Whitfield Diffie and Martin Hellman, and it spun off VeriSign in 1995, although other companies also hold stakes in it.

What does this mean to you? It means that to give your online customers confidence that the credit card numbers they're giving you aren't being stolen over the Internet, you need to support Secure Sockets Layer (SSL) encryption. To do that, you need to purchase a private encryption key from VeriSign. VeriSign charges commercial Web sites $349/year for such a key, which is good for one year, but it also renews those keys for $249/year and offers additional digital keys for the same price.

Anil Pereira, director of consumer and corporate marketing at VeriSign, explains how this works. The company starts by going to the VeriSign Web site and filling out a form. "You provide a whole bunch of data," but the most important pieces are your company's address, the number of your Dun & Bradstreet credit report, the URL of your Web site, and your business' main telephone number. In the process of sending the application, VeriSign generates a key pair and a certificate signing request. These are attached to the company's request. "We then take a public key and cryptographically shrink-wrap that application, and sign it with our digital signature," the VeriSign private key. "This authenticates the information you gave as having come from you."

"There are three things we're authenticating," he says. "First, is your company indeed a company? For that we use Dun & Bradstreet," which maintains and sells business credit reports. "Next, we work with Network Solutions Inc.," which hands out domain names under contract with the National Science Foundation, "to authenticate the company name against the URL."

There's also a third check, since you could have falsely applied for a key under a real company's name, and gotten its D&B number by asking for a credit report on it. "We then do a back-end check, via the telephone, to that person, and authenticate that you're at that company," using the phone number on the D&B report. Each application requires two contacts—a technical contact and an organizational contact—so this call will take a few minutes. Once you're contacted by phone, VeriSign will e-mail you the completed certificate.

Once your server has obtained, and stored, a private key, taking orders is simple. "The brilliance of SSL is that you can put up simple HTML templates, then conduct commerce by simply having a certificate," said Pereira. "You put up a form that captures data and e-mails it to you . . . it's real easy."

When a message is encrypted with SSL, it is scrambled as it flows across the Internet. In practice, what users see is a blue bar at the top of their browser window and a key in one corner of the window, which usually looks broken but now looks whole, with a blue border around it to heighten the icon's visibility.

What if you have a big company, with a lot of servers? You can become your own certificate authority. VeriSign sells a server called VeriSign OnSite that lets you create and store your own private keys for $5,000. Does this mean you can now go into competition with VeriSign? Not exactly. A public key authority needs to have its root keys supported by companies that make browser and server software, which means getting support for your offering (and trust in your good name) from Microsoft and Netscape.

"We issue digital certificates, and we have a broad range of trust services surrounding that," Pereira explained. A public certificate authority, in other words, needs to be trusted by banks, credit reporting agencies, and major software companies, as well as users.

■ PRETTY GOOD PRIVACY

There is another encryption system used on the Internet, called PGP. PGP stands for Pretty Good Privacy (PGP) and was created by software engineer Phil Zimmerman in 1991, who used it to encrypt his own messages and those of friends. What made Zimmerman famous was his willingness

to release a free toolkit on the Internet (web.mit.edu/network
/pgp.html), with which anyone else could create private keys
and encrypt their own messages. The U.S. government, which
fears the mass use of strong encryption as a matter of public
policy, threatened to prosecute Zimmerman for enabling the
export of something that would protect the messages of ter-
rorists, drug dealers, and other criminals, making Zimmerman world famous. (It also spurred enormous demand
for PGP.) In 1996, after the government had decided against
prosecuting, Zimmerman founded PGP Inc. (www.nai.com
/default-pgp.asp) in San Mateo, California, to commercialize
the technology. PGP was acquired by Network Associates in
December 1997.

You can get a number of encryption products from PGP.
These include PGP Personal Privacy for encrypting e-mails
and files you're about to transfer ($39).

In theory, PGP could easily be used in electronic commerce. You can get a private key without using a certificate
authority, and you don't even need a browser to create
an encrypted message—just an e-mail package and the
company's public-domain key-generating software. In practice, PGP is used mostly to protect e-mail and other discrete
transmissions like calls made using Internet telephony
software (www.pgp.com/products/pgp-fone.cgi). Users like
Zimmerman publish their public keys (www.nai.com/products
/security/phil/phil-key.asp), while keeping their private keys
to themselves. PGP sells a server, called the PGP Business Security Suite, which can manage a company's internal use of
digital keys and protect messages before they even reach the
Internet. PGP also sells toolkits for enabling encryption in
local area networks and Unix-based computer systems.

■ SET

The newest security standard in electronic commerce is the
Secure Electronic Transaction (SET) specification, which is

being developed by a consortium headed up by major credit card companies Visa, MasterCard, and American Express, as well as banks, merchants, and other commerce players.

SET is related to SSL in that it uses public and private keys, with the private keys held by a certificate authority. Unlike SSL, SET puts private keys in the hands of both the buyer and the seller in a transaction. What this means is that ordinary users need their own private keys, and need to register those keys, just like servers do now.

Here's how it will work. When a SET transaction is authorized, the user's private key will function as a digital signature that proves the buyer's identity to the seller, and to public payment networks. In practice, it's like signing the charge slip you get at a restaurant. The digital signature proves it's you who ate the meal and accepted the bill. Since buyers can't back out of a SET transaction, claiming they didn't make their purchases, SET transactions will in theory run through the payment system just like those from merchants' terminals.

To make SET work, however, a lot of people need a lot of technical capability they don't have now, Pereira said. "You're taking the entire infrastructure of the payment industry from the physical world and moving it into the electronic world all at once." That means a lot of computer systems have to accept and process digital keys. "There are payment processors, banks, and cardholders, along with merchants who accept credit cards and their banks. SET means everyone in that chain needs a certificate."

Today's credit card processing networks support four-digit bank numbers, four-digit merchant numbers, and 12-digit credit card numbers. (The first four digits on the credit card refer to the bank which issued it.) To process SET, each of those numbers must carry with it a digital signature, proving its individuality, and credit card processing networks must deal with all those digits.

To process SET, you'll need a different certificate than with SSL. Your SSL key changes into a root key from Veri-Sign, and there are intermediate roots to reach a merchant certificate. You're two levels down. In SET there's an industry root, which assigns brand roots, for credit card companies like Visa and Master Card, then bank roots for each bank that issues credit cards, like Citibank, and then individual keys under those roots identifying cardholders and merchants.

Visa trumpeted delivery of the first SET transactions in mid-1997, but the complexity of changing the world's payment networks to accept digital keys, then handing out those keys, means you shouldn't hold your breath, Pereira predicted. By the end of 1998, some large merchants, working closely with their banks, may begin processing SET transactions, and banks which support SET will begin urging their credit holders to get digital credit cards, essentially private keys for which the banks will act as certificate authorities. At the same time, other banks will begin calling on their merchants, urging that they get digital merchant numbers, like the numbers they input into current terminals, but again tied to private keys.

Once enough digital keys are in the hands of merchants and enough digital credit cards are in the browsers of computer users, it will be time to consider implementing SET on your Web site. Most likely, banks will sign agreements with software companies that support electronic commerce, and approach Web-based merchants with those solutions.

In other words, get SET for a sales call.

■ CASE STUDY—VERISIGN

VeriSign (www.verisign.com) has made a niche out of selling digital certificates. The keys to success were focus and scale. The company's Web site was designed from the start to handle millions of digital certificates. It was also designed by security experts. Requests for digital certificates are encrypted using SSL, and the digital certificates themselves are behind firewalls.

In addition to the database, the site must also have extensive links, with automatic searching. Data on a field for a Dun & Bradstreet report must, upon being entered on a form, be found in the background. So must the URL of the party requesting the certificate. Finally, there must be personal follow up, operators who have access to the phone numbers on the forms and can quickly call those numbers to verify identities.

"Keeping the site current also requires constant redesign," says technical webmaster Amy Broski. In the latest redesign, launched late in 1997, three major paths were created through the site, depending on the type of digital ID a user wanted to buy. "That's how we focus our message, based on customers," she says.

It's a challenge to market correctly to different groups, especially when the same person may be a member of more than one group. For instance, a computer systems director may want to trade stocks securely with a personal digital ID. "One of our challenges is marketing to different groups," she says.

The answer is to have product managers focused on those different groups, who can provide the input needed for Broski to design materials appealing to those groups, determine which ones are Web-savvy and interactive, and which put the company's best face forward. The product managers' input, in turn, is based on research conducted on the site, especially a careful analysis of server logs. These track user interests based on the number of visits to different areas of the site. As a result, every visit becomes a market test. "Once someone comes in our front door we can see where they go."

Broski offers two other success secrets. First, there is a clear approval process, controlled by marketing, in all major site decisions. Broski sits in on those meetings. Second, the Webmaster is highly trained, and not just in HTML. "I was trained in other fields, but I come from a Web marketing background. I have been working on the Web since 1993, when I got my doctorate from Columbia. I was also at Oracle for two years before coming to VeriSign. A Webmaster needs to be a jack of all trades . . . not just a technical or marketing person," says Broski.

Part III
Industry Applications

Chapter 9

Business-to-Business

Business-to-business sales are far more complicated than sales made to consumers. There are many reasons for this. Many business products are purchased as parts for other business products, so the relationship in those cases is more like a partnership. Bigger purchases mean bigger discounts. Prices are nearly always negotiable. Also, large businesses have their own computer systems and standards for exchanging invoices such as electronic data interchange (EDI) with which Web sites must integrate in order to do deals.

Despite all this, a number of companies have found opportunity in business-to-business Web sites. Business customers are always highly motivated to save money, so there's less reluctance to look online for savings. Businesses already have computer systems, and many are rebuilding their networks as intranets, based on the same standards—TCP/IP and HTTP—which make up the Web.

The business-to-business Web purchasing market is evolving rapidly. Nets Inc., a company founded just three years ago to give businesses their own home pages on the Internet, has already gone under. Their place has been taken in part by distributors such as Fisher Technology Group and W.W. Grainger. Trade publishers such as Cahners and Penton have entered the market. So have established players in business-to-business commerce such as GE Information Systems and the Thomas Register, which have built their own business mega-sites. For companies looking to buy or sell industrial products, sites like these are a good place to start to find some real business.

Despite all this, there is still ample opportunity in the business-to-business Web site marketplace, as long as you have something to sell that businesses wish to buy.

■ WHAT ARE YOUR GOALS?

If you have goods to sell, if you need to buy goods to make what you sell to consumers, or if you have valuable information to sell to other businesses, you can find a place online. Having a home page, however, is not enough. Linking your key people to their own suppliers, customers, and collaborators via e-mail is more important and simpler. All you need is an Internet connection with enough bandwidth to carry your local network's outside e-mail traffic and either an Internet connection via existing software or Internet e-mail software (a standard part of browsers like Netscape 3.0) on every desktop.

Once you have a connection to the Internet, you want to consider what you show and what you sell to the world. Ask yourself some key questions:

> ➤ Can I put my whole catalog online?
> ➤ What should be my policy on employee use of the Internet?
> ➤ Should I make or buy electronic commerce services?
> ➤ How much of a business transaction can my suppliers and customers really do with me on the Internet? How do they interface with my systems now, and what would change on the Net?

➤ What should I offer free and what information should I charge for?

➤ Whom do I want to link to from my Web pages?

When you have the answers to these questions, you can start to formulate an online budget. Prioritize your goals, estimate the costs of reaching the most important goals, put someone with knowledge in charge of reaching those goals, then get to work.

Remember that the Internet is not just a technology platform. It's also a marketing and business platform. Great Web sites are built with a team approach. Technologists, programmers, marketers, and businesspeople must work together. If you can't bring together four people to make your Web site go, at least have a group from all those disciplines advising your Webmaster, with someone in charge who has the interests of your whole enterprise at its head.

■ WHAT'S THE SETUP?

You don't have to have an intranet in your business to have a successful business-to-business Web site, but it helps. If your network isn't connected to the Internet now, you can make that happen through an Internet Service Provider (ISP) which has a node in your area. A directory such as *Boardwatch Magazine's Directory of Internet Service Providers* (8500 W. Bowles St., Suite 210, Littleton, CO, 80123, (800) 933-6038) costs $9.95/issue. It provides great background on the Internet and lists not only the two dozen or so companies with cross-country "backbone" connections but all the ISPs with connections or *points of presence* in your area code. Many ISPs can host your Web site, some provide electronic commerce services such as transaction processing, and many will provide a bulk rate on Internet e-mail boxes with your company's own domain name or corporate address.

Here are some of the questions you'll need to answer on the way to negotiating a Web hosting or Internet Service Provider contract:

➤ How fast is your fastest line?

➤ What are your "peering" relationships with other backbone providers? Do you have multiple points of access (called multihoming) to the Internet backbone, so if one backbone provider goes down you're not off-line?

➤ How many e-mail boxes can your ISP host for your employees, at what cost?

➤ How long is your commitment to this ISP? At what price? For what kind of line?

➤ Will you be charged the same amount every month no matter how much bandwidth you use? How is your bandwidth use measured?

➤ What support can the ISP provide in designing your Web site? In handling electronic commerce? What does that cost?

You have many choices to make before you sign on the dotted line. You'll want to compare contracts for length, price, and features, just as you would the purchase of any other important business asset. You want to consider whether to have your Web site hardware located in your offices, or in the offices of an Internet Service Provider or Web-site host as well— remember you need 24-hour-a-day, 7-day-a-week coverage wherever you go. Once you have a domain name, an e-mail connectivity, and a place to host your Web site, you build your team and build your site.

■ HOW IS WEB COMMERCE IMPACTING DISTRIBUTION CHANNELS?

In the consumer world, the Web is all about disintermediation, getting rid of the middlemen who stand between the maker of a product and the person who ultimately buys and uses it. The situation is more complex in the business-to-business world. Many products are designed to go inside other products—computer chips designed to go into computers represent one example. Other products, such as industrial machines and tools, are sold to factories for use in making other products. The consumers in both these cases are other businesses.

Information can also be an important product in the business-to-business marketplace. For instance, Aspect Development Inc., Mountain View, California, provides the service of helping electronics designers decide which parts can substitute for other parts in their designs, then how to get to those parts.

■ MRO

Most business-to-business product sales are in the areas of maintenance, repair, and operations, commonly known as MRO. MRO products can range from the simple to the complex, and quantities purchased can range from one to 1 million. Mops and uniforms are MRO. So are machines that wash computer chips.

Every industry has its own MRO needs, which are ongoing. The more you buy, the more you should save on your purchases. There are hundreds of distributors for MRO supplies, but while the Web is one of many factors helping the industry consolidate, it's not eliminating the need for the accounting, inventory, or information, for financing, or for the other back-office needs these companies fulfill. Large MRO distributors such as Grainger.Com and Procure.Net already have extensive Web sites.

The Web does impact the MRO business in many ways. Geographic proximity to your customers is now just a delivery advantage—it doesn't make anyone buy from you. Personal contacts and good salesmanship may no longer be enough. But you can take advantage of the Internet to find your way in MRO distributing:

➤ Specialize in a specific industry to minimize the number of potential competitors.

➤ Offer your customers information vital to their business success, both online and off-line.

➤ Automate, automate, automate. If you provide back-office functions for your customers, you provide value worth paying for.

The Internet can help in all these areas. It can help you research your industry. It can deliver that research, as well as links to your sources, which customers may find valuable. (If it's valuable enough, that industry intelligence becomes a service you can sell, protected by passwords and user names that also help you track your loyal clients.) It can help you stay in touch with customers, and suppliers, through e-mail and conferencing newsgroups.

You can learn all about your customers' problems on the Internet, in other words, then use the Internet to deliver answers to customers and cement your relationship with them. You won't need new technology to accomplish any of this—just time and intelligence.

■ EDI

Electronic data interchange (EDI) is a vital tool in business-to-business transactions, and becomes more vital as your customers get larger. EDI is a set of standards developed in the 1980s specifically to handle business transactions electronically. EDI is used to replace all the paperwork businesses previously generated—invoices, purchase orders, even checks. It prescribes methods for authenticating the identity of companies sending invoices, for proving delivery of goods, and for delivering payment.

GE Information Services is the largest provider of EDI services, but there are other EDI networks as well, like Harbinger Services. Over the last decade, all these companies have built secure networks, and complete solutions, for America's largest companies.

The Internet provides a competitive threat to these companies, but it also offers an opportunity. The Internet, like e-mail, lets EDI networks extend their reach to even the smallest customers and suppliers. General Electric Corp. saved millions of dollars on its own purchasing, extending its own EDI network to small suppliers in this way. Another result was TradeWeb, through which it hopes to offer these savings, for a fee, to other large companies. Through TradeWeb, companies can use GE's EDI network with other companies whose systems support it, and secure e-mail with those suppliers too small to support it.

■ TRADE NETWORKS

The new trade networks offer great opportunities for companies to research their markets, make contacts, and link their home pages to business customers. Penton Design, Engineering, & Manufacturing Network is run by a magazine publisher that competes with Cahners. The site is based on the company's Penton Census, which lists the readers of its 10 magazines. The aim of the directory is to link buyers and sellers, and the company will provide paid links to help its readers do just that.

Manufacturing Marketplace—the heart of Cahners' Manufacturing.Net—is the site of its dozens of industry-specific magazines. But Cahners' parent company, Reed-Elsevier Inc., also owns the Lexis-Nexis service, and puts some of that paid online service's general and industry-specific news on the marketplace site, which requires registration for use.

The marketplace also includes a directory of over 50,000 manufacturers and distributors, Web links to over 3,500 sellers' Web sites, and a searchable buyers' guide with more than 30,000 product categories. The site sells advertising but is also in the process of delivering electronic commerce services through Waypoint Software Inc., a unit of Open Market Inc. specializing in business-to-business catalog software solutions.

TPN Register is a joint-venture between GEIS and Thomas Publishing, publishers of the popular Thomas Register business directory. The Register, a 33-volume green-bound directory with 52,000 different product and service classifications, is the biggest, and oldest, business directory around. The Register also has short descriptions of over 150,000 companies. TPN Register, however, wants to go far beyond offering the Register over the Internet. The company plans to offer EDI and other electronic commerce functions to the Register's on-line advertisers, linking buyers to the clients' Web sites and then performing all the necessary back-office functions.

All the new trade networks can be of great benefit to anyone selling to other businesses on the Web. They can provide links to customers and suppliers, and they can provide solid leads to your Web site.

■ HOW THE WEB SELLS SERVICE

All sorts of business-to-business sales are also based on services, not goods. Accounting, consulting, legal help, and investment banking are just some of the industries whose services are primarily sold to businesses. To get beyond the billboard stage, companies' Web sites need to show other businesses just what they can do for them, and what they've done for others. Law firms' Web sites could detail the cases they've won and the deals they've helped put together in the past, then offer e-mail access directly to the lawyers who won those cases and did those deals, for example. Transaction processing may not be necessary, but decisions must still be made on how much information to offer publicly and in what form.

The advice offered to MRO companies can apply here as well. You can use the Internet to know who your competitors are, to research cases, to find expertise you don't have in-house, and to deliver all sorts of offering letters, sales pitches—even multimedia presentations—to clients and prospects.

■ WHERE ARE WE?

All of these trends are in their infancy. The MRO business, for instance, may be worth as much as $300 billion, but the largest player in the market, W.W. Grainger, still has sales of just $3.5 billion, and most of those are made off-line. Services like accounting, law, and consulting are still mainly in the billboard stage of their Internet evolution.

Your business can use the Web in many ways. You can e-mail suppliers and customers, send invoices through EDI networks, research markets and competitors, all from the comfort of your desk. Your business Web site can provide much more than a billboard. It can be a source of information to your business partners and customers, linking to other sources of information.

Turning such a Web site into a true commerce site, however, requires more. To learn about that, we met with executives running one of the most popular business-to-business Web sites, Procure.Net.

■ CASE STUDY—PROCURE.NET

Procure.Net is owned and operated by Fisher Technology Group, Pittsburgh, Pennsylvania, one of the nation's largest industrial distributors (see Figure 9.1). Bob Grzyb is the company's vice president of marketing. To encourage participation, he said, "We take an 'anchor tenant' concept. An example is the Gage Co., a maker of pipe valves and fittings.

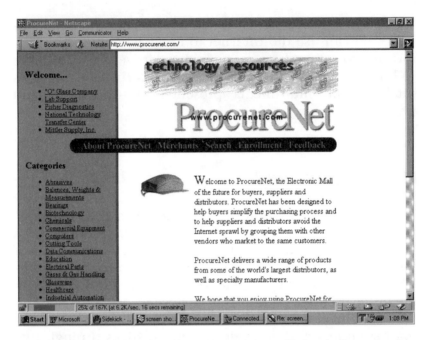

Figure 9.1. Procure.Net is an electronic mall that brings together buyers, sellers, and distributors of manufacturing parts and other products and services.

These large distributors bring users and buyers they're serving to the site. This affords everyone on the supply side the opportunity to have their products and services exposed to that purchasing community." As a result, Procure.Net is a proven traffic generator for its best customers. "Wesco has seen 3 times as much traffic through Procure.Net as their own Web site," he says. The heart of the site, however, is Cornerstone, an EDI package the company spent millions of dollars developing. It's available to any entity in the supply chains served by Procure.Net.

In addition to delivering invoices and purchase orders online, using EDI, Internet e-mail, or fax, Cornerstone offers the front-end electronic cataloging, searching, and retrieval of information. It takes 30 people to maintain the catalogs offered on the site, and these are experts in working with various types of source copy. Whether it's mainframe ASCII data, from a publishing system, or from an SQL database, they convert it to HTML. "We have another group that converts from hard copy . . . if you just have a printed book, they can create the HTML. We offer that service to participating vendors," and large clients can also purchase the software, said Grzyb.

Each vendor on the Procure.Net system gets its own account manager, who can help them present their information in a way that's navigable, clear, and effective. This is not just to help the sellers. "Part of our value is making it simple for purchasers. We try to make it easy for them to navigate and procure. We're doing a lot at our end to improve the experience for the buyer, which has benefits for the vendors," says Grzyb. Fisher has also invested heavily in market research. Grzyb said, "Our results show most people aren't interested in price shopping—they're doing comparative shopping, comparing features of various products."

Many of the costs associated with Procure.Net would have been born by Fisher, even without the Web, in the course of its regular business as an MRO distributor. Market research is needed to help the sellers it represents find buyers. The EDI package can cut costs for those sellers, as well as buyers who might otherwise be calling the company's operators. Moving sales to the Web from the telephone or physical stores can save enormous amounts of money.

"What people want is a way to take costs out of the procurement cycle, and the Web lets them do that," Grzyb continues. "Those who survive will be those who match the needs of the purchaser and the supplier. He who takes the most cost out in that process will survive. We're there to be a more effective supply chain for buyers and sellers. That's our mantra."

The next chapter will take an even more in-depth look at a business-to-business site that's moving its entire operations onto the Web: NECX.

Chapter

NECX: Computer Exchange Brings Buyers and Sellers Together

Electronic commerce is the ATM for the business-to-business market. It's the self-service component.

Henry Bertolon,
president and chief executive officer, NECX

NECX is one of the world's largest independent distributor of semiconductors, network components, and computer products, with annual sales of $400 million. The company intends to maintain that same leadership position in cyberspace with its online marketplace for buyers and sellers of high-tech products that launched on the Web in 1995 (www.necx.com). NECX is a virtual extension of NECX Exchange, the company's global trading business in Peabody, Massachusetts, where 120 NECX buyers and sellers monitor the pricing and availability of more than 200 million semiconductors from over 20,000 sources around the globe. Since its launch, NECX has been considered a research lab for the

entire NECX Exchange, providing the company both technical and marketing feedback necessary to create a successful
online exchange having the size and complexity of the physical model (see Figure 10.1). Some of NECX's accomplish-
ments to date are:

➤ Generates more than $5 million a month in online
orders, with $60 million in online sales in 1997.

➤ Processes an average of 12,000 orders a month.

➤ Repeat business accounts for 60 percent of orders.

Henry Bertolon, founder, president, and chief executive
officer of NECX, has a vision for the online business, and that
is to create the world's largest global online marketplace for
semiconductors, computers, and networking equipment in a

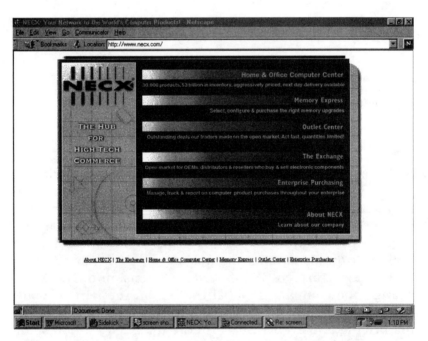

Figure 10.1. The NECX online exchange features more than $1
billion in semiconductors and other computer product inventory.

vertical value-added network (VVAN). "There are many approaches and arguments to the two ways of doing commerce," Bertolon said. "There's the value-added network and the wide, mall approach of carrying many of everything. We want to add value within a vertical area. That's a VVAN. We want to be deep and wide in a particular niche market segment."

Bertolon believes that the ability of the Web to provide a self-service component, whereby individual users can help themselves find the best products, prices, and services, is what will make business-to-business the real money maker of the Internet. Through its ease of use and virtually ubiquitous access in the business environment, the Web allows buyers to go online and get the best deals for purchases they need to make for their companies. NECX, with its two decades worth of experience trading semiconductors, computers, and networking components, wants to act as a middleman in cyberspace to bring this value to Internet users. "Our goal is to have many, many, many distributors and manufacturers listing live inventory with us, so that buyers of those products can come in and find them," says Bertolon. "A distributor of a product may buy a product coming from a competitor, but they do not have to know that. And that's the beauty of the Internet. Many customers want to have anonymity." NECX is important as a Web commerce business for the following reasons:

➤ It takes the commodity exchange model of buying and selling on the open market to the Internet.

➤ It demonstrates the power of the Web for bringing buyers and sellers together.

➤ It introduces a new buying model: aggregate demand.

➤ Like other business-to-business sites, it shows how changes to the distribution channel can encounter initial resistance from key constituents such as manufacturers and sales representatives.

NECX isn't selling nearly as much online as original computer and network equipment manufacturers such as Dell

Computers or Cisco Systems, but that's part of what makes it an interesting case study. As an independent distributor of electronic components, NECX represents no single manufacturer. Rather, it represents original equipment manufacturers and resellers who want to come to a single source to find the best prices on high-volume technical components. Right now, NECX makes its money by buying electronic components and computer products from suppliers, marking up prices, and reselling the products to customers.

For this kind of high-volume business, the Web is the perfect vehicle for opening up NECX's inventory of goods to a global marketplace at a low cost. However, while that model has worked pretty well for NECX and has provided some good feedback for future development, the site still isn't profitable after four years and a $10 million investment.

"We have another $10 million to spend," says Bertolon, a highly energetic, articulate business executive with a passion for technology. NECX will spend this next $10 million re-engineering its site, with the intention of flip-flopping its model from the selling to the buying side. It plans to introduce a new model of buying based on aggregate demand, in which users with demand for a specific product can bid on prices based on volume purchasing, and get a better deal.

Bertolon has taken NECX through several generations, beginning in 1987 with a floppy disk version of the service to the current status of merging NECX with the physical Exchange.

■ FROM THE FLOOR TO THE ONLINE STORE

To understand the online business of NECX, it helps to understand how the Exchange works. NECX Exchange, in business since 1980, is located in the same building that houses NECX at Four Technology Drive in Peabody, 45 minutes outside of Boston just off Route 128.

Dominating the center of the huge trading floor is a large three-dimensional screen, which hangs directly over

an area called the pit and flashes current pricing and availability information on computer, semiconductor, and
networking products from 20,000 different manufacturers
worldwide in red, green, and orange lights. A ticker runs
across the bottom of the screen with product and pricing
alerts such as this: "Toshiba is due to drop pricing on some
of their notebooks by May 1," keeping traders abreast of the
most current information. The data on pricing and part
availability comes into NECX from manufacturers, distributors, and other sources around the globe, in a variety of
formats, including the following:

➤ 3,000 faxes a day.
➤ 2,500 telephone calls a day.
➤ 50 different electronic data feeds from manufacturers.

This results in more than 10,000 new product and pricing
items keypunched daily into an Oracle database tracking
more than 1.7 million individual products.

This database is the heart of NECX's business, and it's
arguably the most comprehensive in the industry. When
high-tech OEMs such as IBM and AT&T need to find electronic components such as DRAMs or EPROMs, and they
can't order them directly from suppliers such as National
Semiconductor or Texas Instruments because the vendors
are out of stock or prices are too high, they can turn to manufacturers' distributors who keep the parts in stock or can
find them elsewhere. One alternative is to turn to franchise
distributors such as Arrow Electronics or Avnet EMG that re-
sell parts from specific component manufacturers, or they
can turn to independent distributors such as NECX that
track pricing and availability for components all over the
world, not just those made by specific manufacturers.

This database really started building momentum in the
mid-1980s, when NECX started tracking not just pricing and
availability of electronic components directly from manufacturers, but also excess inventory that OEMs had. For example,
if an OEM in Singapore ordered 50,000 semiconductors from

a manufacturer and needed to get rid of 20,000 because of a change in production, it could send the information to NECX, which would keep it in its database. Because NECX tracks order history by part number, that data would be available if another buyer came in looking for 20,000 of those specific parts, which it may not be able to find in the manufacturer's database. And that is the real benefit of NECX's independent stature. Each day, more than 160 NECX traders talk to roughly 5,000 buyers and sellers to match up their needs. But they're limited in terms of sheer resources. In extending this operation to the Web, NECX wants to leverage its massive database and provide its community of buyers and sellers with an easier to use, self-service format. But with the complexity of the business, it has taken NECX years to put the pieces together, and it's now poised to launch entirely new ways of conducting business. Along the way, the company has learned some valuable lessons in what makes for a successful e-commerce business.

■ EARLY E-COMMERCE

NECX was an online pioneer, launching Hard Facts on Disk, an online catalog accessible via a dial-up connection that was distributed to users over diskette in 1987. Containing pricing and specifications on over 15,000 products located in NECX's inventory, Hard Facts was distributed to NECX's buyers, including OEMs and resellers. The proprietary software, written by NECX programmers with Clipper software, a relational database tool, and C programming routines, linked users to NECX's database, where they could access product and pricing information. But if they wanted to order anything, they had to pick up the phone and call NECX.

While experimenting with Hard Facts, NECX uncovered a new use for the system that eventually led to the launch of the next phase of the product: Buyers trading their own products. After dialing into NECX's server, the system would hang for a few seconds or longer. NECX decided to use this time to display a screen on which users could communicate with each other and source products. For example, a buyer at an IT company might post information about laptop computers his firm manufactured. Using this tool, NECX was able to develop a database that stored information about not only its sellers' products but its buyers' products as well. And thus was born Trader Desk, Phase II of the online system that launched in 1989.

With Trader Desk, NECX learned a valuable lesson about e-commerce nearly a decade ago that some of its Web competitors are just now starting to find out: Accessible, up-to-date product and pricing information is often a deterrent to some manufacturers and distributors that want to keep the supply chain intact.

"Distributors didn't want products with pricing up on the network," said Bertolon. "Ingram Micro didn't want their potential customers to see that they wanted $300 for a printer, when that same printer was being sold somewhere else for $280." Therefore, he added, "They were reluctant to give us their inventory. They just wanted us to show the goods."

NECX realized it needed to develop a way to link to manufacturers' databases to get the most current pricing information, creating a system that would search for products based on price and show users the lowest cost products without doing a side-by-side comparison. In this way, it could protect its manufacturer's interests, and boost its own role as a middleman by providing a searching service for its customers. The next step in the evolution of the online store was Desktop Channel, incorporating these features and launching in 1990.

Desktop Channel was actually a separate company that was launched by Bertolon, and became the predecessor to the online marketplace. The idea was to create an online link to manufacturers' data, so users could shop for products. The software was again a dial-up proprietary connection distributed via disk to NECX's customers, and initially NECX linked with only one distributor, Ingram. While the system was an interesting prototype that eventually grew into a much more comprehensive catalog, initially it allowed buyers to purchase only from Ingram. Eventually, NECX added more distributors, and "it came to the point where the Desktop Channel was the whole model," said Bertolon. The Desktop Channel tracked more than 1 million specifications on products from over 20,000 manufacturers. The software also provided a fax-back service that allowed users to order products online, so all they had to do was click on an item and press "fax me," and the fax server would call up the manufacturer and request a document number for the order. Another feature was the ability for manufacturers to provide product data sheets that they scanned into the Desktop Channel database that automatically faxed spec sheets to potential buyers if they requested the information. While these features may not seem very sophisticated compared to today's point-and-click Web technology, what's important is the following two points:

1. NECX utilized existing technology in innovative ways that gave it an edge when the Web finally came into being in 1983.

2. NECX looked at ways to bring buyers and sellers together in new ways to trade more effectively.

■ NECX TO THE WEB

By 1993, Bertolon said he'd invested about $2.5 million in the Desktop Channel, and had only generated between $2 million to $3 million in revenue. "I was losing money," he said. Then, things started to happen with the World Wide Web. Marc Andreessen developed the Mosaic browser, an easy-to-use Web navigational tool that eventually became the Netscape Navigator, while he was a grad student at the University of Illinois, and suddenly the Web had a front end.

Just as suddenly, the Internet Shopping Network launched with an online computer store, and NECX had a competitor.

"They hadn't even been in the business," said Bertolon. "We made a decision to get up on the Web." NECX hired EIT, a Web development firm that had built the Internet Shopping Network site, and the Desktop Channel was up on the Web in four months under the NECX name. From the beginning, Bertolon knew the online catalog was going to be a research laboratory to figure out how to eventually move the entire NECX Exchange online. Originally containing just the computer networking products, which make up just a small percent of NECX's total business, the service evolved over several years from basic price searching to a sophisticated product center.

"We wanted to learn about the Web without exposing our core business (semiconductors)," said July Ashley, MIS director at NECX.

Bertolon adds, "NECX is the embryonic lab that's served as the development piece for getting NECX capable, both technically and with regard to the infrastructure in terms of the skill sets, to be able to engage in the self-service component of electronic commerce. We are totally an end-to-end electronic commerce solution. We don't touch anything." The electronic commerce self-service model is the ideal buying mechanism in the business-to-business world, Bertolon believes, because it's the cheapest, fastest, and most efficient way for large companies to shop for products, particularly competitively priced computer products. Using NECX, buyers can indicate what products they're interested in, and get not only the best prices, but also detailed product descriptions, reviews, industry articles, and comparison tools.

While NECX is targeting businesses, it's had its share of home consumers visit the site, and this is another one of the lessons it has learned in operating an electronic commerce business: Make sure you define your target market, but be prepared to deal with all kinds of users. "One of the challenges when you go out into the cyber environment, with millions of eyeballs, and you don't restrict them from coming, is you're going to get all kinds of comers," said Bertolon. "You're going to get a lot of consumers who buy a $50 piece of software or a $200 printer. And while they're good customers, we want to build a community of people that want to buy and sell in volume."

With this in mind, NECX created different areas of its site to cater to its various types of business customers. When buyers come into NECX, they can enter the following areas:

> ➤ Home and Office Computer Center, the heart of NECX, with pricing and product information on more than 30,000 computer products, networking products, and software.
> ➤ Enterprise Purchasing Network, an interactive ordering system designed for high-volume IT buyers.
> ➤ Exchange, the online global marketplace that tracks the movement of worldwide inventory for semiconductors, network equipment, and computer products.
> ➤ Memory Express, for ordering memory upgrades.
> ➤ Outlet Center, for end-of-life products.

■ HOME AND OFFICE COMPUTER CENTER

Once in the Computer Center, buyers can search for specific products by entering key words into a field, or clicking on one of several product categories such as desktops & servers, network hardware & software, or printers & supplies to go to product listings. Across the top of the screen, NECX displays banners on featured products, some of which are paid ads and some of which are products that NECX wants to merchandise. "We don't allow all of our prime real estate to be sold," said Brian Marley, business development manager of NECX, referring to ad space on the site's key pages. "Then you lose control of your merchandising strategy."

Moreover, "Manufacturers who have ad dollars to spend don't necessarily have the products you want to feature, and the leaders may not need to spend ad dollars," added Marley, who has been with NECX since the launch of Hard Facts on Disk.

NECX's product line managers decide which products to feature on the Computer Center home page to drive traffic to different areas of the site. Once on the product page, users are presented with a detailed product description, specifications, features, and pricing information written and compiled by NECX's online content editors. Or users can go to a category such as printers and see a listing of all products in that category with pricing and availability. If they want to order, they can do so online.

The interactive home page and individual product pages are updated daily. Each morning, product managers, editorial staff, and Web site designers hold a "power hour" in the NECX "playpen," a large cubicle area where the four-person Web development team works, to decide which products to feature and what changes to make on key pages. Then, throughout the day, individual product line managers meet with NECX Web designers to implement specific changes to products within their lines.

Marley said one of the keys to NECX's success is doing a good job merchandising products. The product managers work with 10 online content editors to make sure they have enough product information to write a detailed description, that they have high-quality images of products, and that the copy on the featured products displays reads like compelling ad copy. "We need to provide all the answers that a customer needs to know," said Marley. "If you can't do that, everyone will come off-line."

To get customer feedback, NECX includes its phone number on the site and encourages customers to call with questions. Some users want to order over the phone rather than online. But the most important thing NECX is learning from its call-in line is why people aren't buying online. For example, they might be having difficulty setting up their online account or they might have questions about security. "We might need to do more handholding," said Marley.

■ ENTERPRISE PURCHASING NETWORK

The Enterprise Purchasing Network, launched in late 1996, is an interactive ordering system that's designed for high-volume buyers. Using EPN, buyers have more control and management over the ordering process. Here are some of the features:

➤ Credit limit authorization that lets companies set purchasing ranges for buyers.

➤ Standardized product lists that limit buyers' product category choices.

➤ Buyer access monitoring that lets users set up user IDs, passwords, and profiles.

➤ Product purchasing reporting that provide purchase order history and ability to download spreadsheets.

➤ Broadcasting feature that lets companies send budgets or billing information to multiple buyers across an enterprise.

➤ Interactive mail, which notifies NECX of account issues.

The thrust of EPN is that it manages and tracks all of an enterprise's technology purchases.

■ EXCHANGE

The Exchange is one of the newest section of NECX, launched in mid-1997. The goal is to automate the core of NECX's business, which is the semiconductor marketplace.

In addition to searching for the best prices on semiconductors and other electronic components, users can sell their own inventory on the open market by indicating how much of a certain product they have in stock, at what price and for how long. Functioning as a true open marketplace for these products, NECX Exchange uses the Web to let it users communicate with other buyers and sellers around the world.

■ HOW THE SYSTEM WORKS

The entire NECX site is hosted on Netscape Commerce Server software running on Sun Sparc servers. The Computer Center site was built almost entirely from scratch by a team of in-house developers, utilizing C programming, CGI, and PERL scripts. "Everything was done by brute force," said Ashley, the MIS director. "There were no tools."

However, with the launch of Exchange last year, NECX is taking advantage of newer tools, such as a Net Dynamics java code generator. "The industry has come a long way technology-wise," said Ashley. "Now there are build and buy decisions."

The central features of the site are the searching and ordering mechanisms, which interface with databases of NECX, manufacturers, and distributors. Here's how the systems works: To order products in the Computer Center, customers must first register by setting up a user profile, which contains authorization information and purchasing limits. To merely search, they don't have to register. Depending upon which part of the site they're in, buyers can perform a range of activities, and the system accesses and displays information from a variety of sources in real time.

When searching for products in the store, customers can search by exact product name, key words, category, subcategory, or by clicking on department boxes, as well as side-by-side comparisons. One search feature is called specification search, and it lets users specify dozens of parameters. For example, a customer shopping for a bar-code printer can specify price, speed, resolution, media width, and other specs, as well as request product reviews, interface ports, available fonts, and normal or reverse font printing. And those are just some of the parameters. NECX uses its own search engine to get information from an Oracle database, which contains up-to-the-minute pricing and parameter information that's fed into the system continuously from the sources described earlier in this chapter.

Another key feature of the site is the ability to dynamically create HTML pages, so that in addition to reflecting all the current pricing and specification information that's coming in from manufacturers and distributors, product pages also contain current product reviews, updates to product descriptions, and other changes that are continuously being made by NECX Web designers.

When a user submits an order, several things happen. First, if it's a credit card transaction, NECX sends the information over EDI to LitleNet, the credit card processing network, and once the transaction is approved it sends the order to the distributor's warehouse closest to the buyer's location. In addition, it gives the buyer current shipping rates for UPS, Fed Ex and other delivery services, and lets the distributor know how the buyer wants to ship the product. The order is touched by two people: the person who takes it from the warehouse shelf out to the loading dock, and the delivery person.

The search mechanism in Exchange is much more barebones than in the Computer Center, partly because it hasn't been up as long and therefore has not evolved as the store has, and partly because of the nature of the semiconductor business.

As opposed to the computer and networking business, where corporate buyers are shopping for complex products based on a number of factors such as price, speed, quality, color, system requirements, and subjective factors as well, the semiconductor business is fairly straightforward, with manufacturers usually shopping for a specific product based on price. Therefore, the systems built to handle the searching and shopping for these products are entirely different. "In that industry, they only talk part numbers," says Ashley. "It's at a very low level." Therefore, OEMs looking for a specific part just type in the number, such as "74-LS02," and the NECX system will search its Oracle database for pricing and availability, displaying the information in text format. There are no flashy pictures or product reviews or product descriptions, although in time those features may be added.

The ordering mechanism of Exchange isn't nearly as evolved, either. In fact, at the time of this book's printing there was no electronic transaction mechanism in place. If buyers want to order parts, they have to call in or e-mail the orders.

■ RE-ENGINEERING THE SITE

In late 1998, NECX was planning a redesign of its site that included the following new functions:

1. Catalog management.
2. Salesforce automation.
3. Enterprise resource package (ERP) integration.

The redesign is based on a totally re-engineered architecture that includes a 100 megabyte Ethernet backbone capable of two-way full-motion video, Internet telephony, and integration with back-end databases. But even with the enhanced site, NECX executives envision moving no more than 35 percent of its sales online, because they still see a role for human interaction. "You have to be willing to service customers in whatever space they want to be serviced," says Bertolon. "We're dealing in an open market environment, where the business rules are changing all the time. They may never be so defined that all transactions can take place without some human assistance," he said. Not only that, but buyers placing high-volume orders may not want to do so online, and might require the assistance of a trader.

With this in mind, NECX is incorporating features that will allow buyers to search for specific electronic components and other computer equipment online, but interact over the system via Internet telephony and other technology with an NECX trader when they get to the point where they need to negotiate the final pricing. This is the salesforce automation piece of the re-engineered system. It has not yet been implemented.

Here's an example of how the interaction would work. A buyer might be looking for 50,000 semiconductors, and be willing to pay 80 cents apiece. After entering his bid into the system, he might see that a manufacturer in Taiwan that wants to remain anonymous has 27,000 of the semiconductors, but wants $1 apiece. At that point, the buyer could interact by phone with an NECX trader to see if the trader could find the rest of the components for him at a price that is right.

"When a user is sitting on the other end and they have questions, it's not very good for the user to type in a question and get an e-mail back. If you're buying to keep a factory going, e-mail won't cut it," said Bertolon. "People want answers now." And NECX is betting that answering those questions and getting the right products to buyers at the right prices is a great way to maintain a global edge online.

The next chapter will take a look at traditional retail business on the Web.

Traditional Retail Business on the Web

If you already have a thriving retail business, you have some complications your Web-based competitors don't have. For starters, you probably already have a computer system, and ways of handling orders, inventory, and transactions, which must be adapted to the Web for you to be efficient there. You also have a corporate culture that may be incompatible with the Web.

These are not small problems. Whether your existing store is physical or a mail-order operation, you face the hard work of integrating that operation with the vagaries of the Web. It's good to consider some of those problems before continuing. There are many challenges to face before adding the Web to your operations. Some are technical, others are not. They include:

➤ 24 × 7 customer service requirements.

➤ Communicating goals between the Web operation and those responsible for the physical store.

➤ Communicating sales offers between the Web operation and the physical store.

➤ Transferring your marketing effort to the Web.

➤ Adjusting your marketing effort to the Web.

➤ Competition for resources between physical store efforts and the Web.

➤ Integration of back-end processes, inventory, and transaction systems.

We will examine each of these issues:

■ 24 × 7 CUSTOMER SERVICE REQUIREMENTS

Your store has fixed hours. Most likely, you're not open 24 hours a day, 7 days a week. But Web stores must be open all the time. How do you provide the same level of support to a Web customer at 7 A.M. Sunday morning as you do at 3 P.M. Monday afternoon?

Maintaining the Web site itself is the simplest problem to solve. If your store is large enough, you might host it yourself, using existing information systems (IS) personnel and budgets. Most likely, however, the IS department won't want to give away that budget. For that reason, even large stores like to locate their Web sites with a professional Web host or internet service provider (ISP).

There's another problem: maintaining human contact with your customer all night. If you're taking orders by phone, there may be an answer for you. Vocaltec (www .vocaltec.com) now offers software to integrate Internet Telephony into your existing customer-service lines. A user on your Web site whose computer supports Internet telephony would click on an icon, and the phone would ring in your operations center. Again, if your store is large enough, you may be able to train one of your operators to take such calls. In October 1997, Vocaltec said it would work with Dialogic (www.dialogic.com) and Executone (www.executone.com) to sell its solution to service bureaus.

■ COMMUNICATION BETWEEN WEB AND PHYSICAL STORE STAFFS

Stores and retail chains that have opened Web sites say there's one good way to make sure your Web store doesn't compete with your physical store, while still having a chance to succeed: Start small.

That's what Macy's (www.macys.com) did. The company launched its Web site from a single outlet in San Francisco with a few select items. When orders came in, a clerk would physically go into the building, take them off a shelf, and ring them up on a cash register. To utilize this manpower more effectively, the store launched a personal shopper service, offering to check the store for specific types of gifts, in specific price ranges, in response to e-mails. The success of this program enabled the Web store to get the funding necessary to integrate its computer operations with the rest of the store, and slowly expand the line of goods it carried.

Small stores that start their Web business slowly can adapt to the nature of the Web at their own pace. The St. Louis Dart Shop (www.cloverka.com/catalog) is a good example. Owner Michael Stafos admits he took a big risk in launching his Web site, spending $5,000 to $8,000 for design, hosting, and credit card processing. While most of his business had previously been done on a wholesale basis, with catalogs sent to dart clubs and bars, he found most of his Web customers were buying in small quantities. But he did take enough time to adapt to that change, along with the variation in where his customers came from. While his physical store draws customers from the metropolitan area, and his paper catalog draws customers from around the country, he found his Web store drew customers from around the world. (He also found himself ordering goods to stock his shelves more often—this was an easy change to make.)

In both these cases, the key to making the store work was in letting someone familiar with the physical operation devote their full attention to the Web, then growing the business in response to customer demand. Investing too far ahead of customer demand is a sure way to spur resentment between the staff of your physical store and that of your Web store.

■ COMMUNICATING GOALS

For a small merchant like Michael Stafos, communicating between the Web store and the physical store is not a problem. But what if you have a large store, with budgets, bureaucracies, and chains-of-command? Again, the Macy's example is instructive. That business was able to grow organically, in response to customer demand and sales. The operation was handled far from its New York headquarters—in San Francisco, in fact. The budget was modest and as it grew—with increasing demands on other Macy's computer systems—so did control of the site from the central office. But the bottom-line success of the site helped shield it from the bureaucratic backbiting which might have otherwise characterized its growth.

Problems can develop when a store puts too big a bet on the Web, too quickly. When executives of Wal-Mart (www .wal-mart.com) saw that Web commerce was growing, top executives of the company brought in leaders throughout the industry to see how they could dominate the field. Their goal was simple—to dominate Web commerce as it dominated small-town commerce. After careful consideration, Microsoft was chosen to bring its new Commerce Server to life at Wal-Mart, integrating the whole company's operations under Windows NT. Did everyone live happily ever after? They haven't yet. A variety of problems plagued the development, which turned into a herculean task. Where Wal-Mart originally hoped to create separate sites for its Wal-Mart and Sam's Club warehouse stores, that plan had to be abandoned. The site, when it was finally launched, was much simpler than originally forecast, with just a selection of the company's products, and it cost much more. At last report, however, Wal-Mart was making progress, this time in the specialized niche of books.

The lesson here should be clear. The communication of goals should come from the top, they should be clear, but they should also be easily achievable.

➤ Communicating Sales Offers

Unless your Web store has a separate set of inventory from your physical store—unless you physically separate Web and physical operations—it's best to let your store's buyers and your business' needs control what goes on sale online.

This is what major publishers of paper catalogs have done. L.L. Bean (www.llbean.com) and Lands End (www.landsend.com) both centralized control of their Web development within their existing operations. They refused to go online until they could deliver an "experience" that would be familiar to readers of their paper catalogs. L.L. Bean, like Wal-Mart, chose to do this with a major vendor, in this case IBM. What was different? Partly it was the smaller scale of the L.L. Bean catalog, compared to that of Wal-Mart's. Partly it was the fact that IBM was already L.L. Bean's major computer systems vendor, so there were existing relationships which could be brought to the Web effort. Partly it was because L.L. Bean, with IBM's advice, started its online business modestly, with a selection of items. But within a few months, the cataloguer was able to offer an increasingly large portion of its inventory online—even offer sales items online before they were printed in the catalog. What can we learn from all this? Placing items on sale comes from a careful mix of buying and inventory control. If you have a successful physical store, leave control of sales with the experts. Your Web staff may offer to use the site for selling small quantities of close-outs—bottom-line success will deliver the confidence to go further.

■ TRANSFERRING MARKETING EFFORTS TO THE WEB

This is where the Web can quickly get away from you. The Web is different from the physical world. It offers ample opportunities for doing things differently. There are many technologies, like Shockwave and streaming video. It offers a different audience from the physical world, sometimes with startling different demographics. Web consumers are wealthier, tech-savvy, and skew more toward male than average consumers. They demand interactivity. They're easily bored. The storeowners we talked with, however, said that it is easy to let the differences between the virtual and the physical world lead you astray. Instead of listening to your Web staff or your in-store staff, listen to your customers. Offer customers the chance to send you e-mails, not messages to the webmaster from the main page but commercial messages on every page. If your Web store has departments, offer users the chance to e-mail department heads with questions from each of those pages. They may request specific items, or they may send useless "flame" mail. Separate one from the other, and use the first as an opportunity, both to make sales and to spur the investigations of buyers.

If you are prepared to move some of your marketing efforts to the Web, be prepared for a struggle, and make sure you're committed to that struggle. That was the decision made by Barnes and Noble (www.barnesandnoble.com), which went online with great fanfare in the summer of 1997. The company's management decided that its Web-based competitor, Amazon.com, was a serious threat to the entire company's future. So Barnes and Noble not only invested heavily in the Web site, with a staff that learned the Web's technical capabilities, but also invested heavily in Web-based marketing, with exclusive deals signed with search engines, online services, and other major sites. The jury is still out on whether the effort will prove profitable, but the chain is more committed to achieving a dominant market share than a profit in the short-term.

■ ADJUSTING YOUR MARKETING EFFORTS TO THE WEB

The Web is different from the physical world. You bring in customers differently, you serve them differently. Does that mean you need a new marketing message? Not necessarily.

Many businesses have found that simply integrating their Web address into their other advertising messages can be a powerful lure to customers. The danger lies in luring surfers before you're ready to serve them—with merchandise, with commerce, and with interactivity (at least e-mail). This was common in 1995, especially with technology-related companies such as Bell Atlantic (www.bellatlantic.net), which erected a very plain vanilla site at www.ba.net, then put the URL in all of its ads to show how advanced the company was.

In contrast, integrating your Web advertising with other media can deliver a big payoff. Take the example of Goodyear (www.goodyear.com), for instance. The company's Web site was designed to do real business with password-protected sections for government customers and dealers. But global Web site manager Rob Elder also put together a virtual "tour" of the company's famous blimp. Traffic was slow until an American League Championship Series game between the Cleveland Indians and Baltimore Orioles. The company put lights on the blimp with the site's URL, and gave the announcers some copy mentioning the blimp tour. "Our traffic zoomed through the roof in the three hours after that announcement, and 80 percent of the visitors suddenly wanted to see the blimp," he recalled.

There is an important lesson here. Integrating your Web site into your marketing efforts can bring great results, but only if you have done your homework and created a pay-off for visitors.

■ COMPETITION FOR RESOURCES BETWEEN PHYSICAL STORE EFFORTS AND THE WEB

Should you just chuck your physical store and put all your chips on the Web? Probably not. Does that mean your Web efforts will be constantly competing for assets against your physical efforts? Perhaps.

Communications is the key, according to Chris Sinton, director of the popular Cisco Connection (www.cisco.com) site (see Chapter 3). "The business management of our site comes from corporate marketing," he says, but "I have standing meetings with the technical people." If you sell your products to other businesses, as Cisco does, and create a partnership between the Web staff and your other marketing people, then the Web can quickly enhance your bottom line by transferring sales to a lower-cost channel. This has been discovered not only by Cisco, but by other technology manufacturers like Dell Computer (www.dell.com) and Compaq Computer (www.compaq.com). Problems are most likely to occur if your business is, in fact, a sales channel.

If you're a store or a distributor, you have many employees whose jobs depend on interaction with people leading to sales. There are two roads to success here. You could commit to the Web from the top of your organization, and separate that development from the rest of the company's business—as in the L.L. Bean and Barnes & Noble examples—or start small, as Macy's did. There is risk in the first instance, as Wal-Mart found. L.L. Bean is privately held, while Barnes and Noble justified its expense as a defense of its niche against a powerful Web competitor, Amazon.com (www.amazon.com). The only risk in the latter case is if a direct competitor goes heavily into the Web first, and succeeds.

Integration of back-end processes, inventory, and transaction systems may be the biggest technical headache you'll face in building a Web business. The bigger your business and the more extensive its pre-Web computer operations, the bigger the challenge becomes.

Starting small can ease these problems, giving you time to perform some functions manually as your transaction volume grows. The growing transaction volume can then justify buying (and installing) software which links to transaction processors and your back-end accounting packages. Scott Eckert, director of Dell Online, had to deal with a legacy system of Tandem mainframes in launching his Web store, which now sells $5 million in computers a day. He used a program called NetWeave to transfer the sales and inventory data between his Web site, which was written with Next's WebObjects, and the mainframe. He wasn't just moving sales data into the Tandem, however, he was moving prices and configuration data out of the Tandem, and putting it live on his site. Thus, he linked the Tandem through NetWeave to an SQL database, which customers could then access through WebObjects. The result was Dell's Configurator, a program that lets users create, or configure, a computer directly from the site, order it online, and get delivery in just a week.

The cost of integrating your Web store with your back-end systems will depend on many factors, including:

➤ The complexity of the back-end systems.

➤ The willingness of the vendors of those systems to support TCP/IP and HTML standards.

➤ Your desire to integrate Web standards into your operations through the creation of an in-house intranet (local networks based on Internet standards).

You will also need to consider each of the following integration procedures as separate projects:

> ➤ Integration with payment networks and payment processing.
> ➤ Integration with inventory and delivery systems.
> ➤ Integration with accounting systems.
> ➤ Integration with communication systems.

Depending on the size of your company, each of these steps may involve a different system and require a different solution. The best solution offered by the Web store managers we interviewed for this book is: You don't have to do it all at once. You don't have to put all your inventory online with the launch of your Web site. You can enter transactions into computers manually until their volume justifies another approach. You may only succeed modestly, but that's better than failing spectacularly.

■ CASE STUDY—FINGERHUT: ANDY'S GARAGE

Most visitors to Andy's Garage (www.andysgarage.com) don't know they're really entering the world of Fingerhut, a $2 billion database-marketing corporation that publishes dozens of print catalogs. That's fine with Jane Westlind, the company's manager of electronic commerce and manager of the garage (see Figure 11.1). "We're treated as an entirely separate entity," she says, within the company as well as without. "We're positioning it differently from our base business."

That was Fingerhut's intention long before it opened the site in October 1995. "Andy's was formed when some of our executives were brainstorming on what we could do with the Internet. We wanted to go beyond cutting and pasting catalog pages. We decided to take what we have here,

Figure 11.1. Andy's Garage offers shoppers bargain-basement prices on goods from jewelry to bedroom furniture.

excess merchandise, and turn it into an opportunity. "Liquidation online takes advantage of the Internet's flexibility. It's inefficient to mail out an excess catalog. The online environment permits us to be more flexible and immediate."

The Web site launched modestly, with just a few people in a basement office, which hosted as well as posted the data on the site. "Garage Sale is quick, it's immediate, it's a retail presence only, and it's first-come, first-serve, with items changing daily," she says. Interaction with customers is mainly via e-mail, and the site posts highlights from that traffic regularly in a section it calls "Ask Andy."

Westlind learned early from tracking e-mail that Web users are very quick with both praise and blame. "Their expectations are extremely high—they'll tell us when they're unhappy. If we are selling something like a bow-and-arrow, we'd get flames from vegetarians. We commit to shipping orders in 14 days, and even though we make that statement our customers are really looking for the shipment sooner . . . the expectation is you may have said 14 days, but where is it? At the same time, they're very loyal," she said. If they're happy with their first visit, they'll come back. If they're happy with their first purchase, they'll come back again and again. But they're also very diverse, Westlind learned. Some were anxious to get a good price on that bow-and-arrow, while others were angry to see it offered. Some people would shop for gifts, others in support of their hobbies. Some were interested in any kind of collectible, others were looking for specific types of items.

A year after the successful launch of the site, Westlind and her colleagues held a series of meetings to consider what they could do to improve the site. The first step, they realized, should be integrating Andy's transactions more completely with Fingerhut's internal computer systems. Ron Peterson, a group manager for systems development with Fingerhut, managed that transition. "Our back-end systems already had payment processing systems," he said. "All we had to do was take the information we captured via the Internet and pass it from our Unix-based Web environment to our IBM mainframe." The key to unlocking that puzzle, he found, was IBM's MQ Series software. "It resides on both Unix and the mainframe," he says. MQ is essentially a messaging system, but there were also different data formats to worry about.

Peterson had to find a way to turn character-based data from the Web site into a structured query record for the mainframe. Worse, the Web form is written in C++, while mainframe programs were written in Cobol. "We went through a learning curve," he admits. "We were the first application area here that used MQ." The whole process took five months. But the sales success of Andy's Garage, and the site's ability to move liquidation merchandise at low cost, justified the investment. "It most certainly is a cost savings opportunity for us."

Now, Peterson and Westlind can face the future of their site with confidence. "We wouldn't have integrated if we didn't feel this was a long term opportunity," Peterson says. There's an important lesson here: Web sites should justify their expenses, especially integration expenses. When they do, they'll get willing cooperation from other departments.

Where's Andy's going next? To personalization, Westlind says. After looking carefully at her site and users, Westlind decided that rules-based personalization was the way to go, and that Broadvision offered the right tools. It ran on her Netscape Commerce Server, and it worked with her Oracle database. In addition, "They provide users with tools and objects to do as much or as little personalization as we want."

It took over three months to implement the Broadvision server—the project was delayed while Fingerhut waited for a new release of the software. Westlind found she needed C++ programmers, object-oriented programmers, and a staff with good database skills to make it work. "We also got some help from Broadvision," she said. "At any time we had three or four people, both ours and theirs, working on the project."

The result of this investment is that Andy's Garage is ready to support Fingerhut in two ways—through its own profitable sales volumes and by selling merchandise at a profit that would otherwise be sold at a loss. Volumes have even grown to the point that Westlind is talking about hiring a separate buyer for the site, who would look for close-out merchandise, buy it in quantity, and bring it online for sale.

Chapter

Selling Big-Ticket Items

In the last few chapters, we've seen how you can use the Web to sell just about anything that can be purchased using a credit card. But can you use the Web for selling something more expensive, like a car or a house?

Yes, you can. The integration problems are different, and the cost of entry may be higher if you're to truly do commerce online, but there are companies succeeding in these areas, and you could be one of them.

■ THE DIFFERENCE BETWEEN BUYING AN AIRLINE TICKET AND A CAR ONLINE

Using airline tickets and cars, let's consider the differences when buying such items:

> ➤ *Financing:* Airline tickets can go on a credit card. While some people hold platinum cards with limits that can handle a car purchase, most do not. Holders of premium plastic didn't get their wealth by paying 20 percent on a car loan.

➤ *Insurance:* Car and insurance purchases usually go hand-in-hand. While many purchasers have an existing policy and a relationship with an agent, not all do.

➤ *Taxes:* You can sell a cushioned car seat cover across a state line over the Internet and probably avoid paying sales taxes. With cars or houses, the taxman cometh—you must account for both sales tax and property tax. Tax rates vary widely by jurisdiction.

➤ *Delivery charges:* The actual price of a new car will vary depending on where it's bought. Japanese cars sold near a Pacific seaport will cost less than those bought in Maine. Even the price of American cars will vary depending on how far they have to travel to reach the buyer.

➤ *Physical examination:* Few people will buy a car or a home without seeing it and kicking the tires. At the very least, most will want a test-drive of the model they want. If the car is to be bought used, they'll likely have to get inside the actual car they're buying. While you can offer a "virtual tour" of a home or model, homebuyers don't buy sight unseen, either.

➤ *Physical delivery:* UPS doesn't deliver cars or houses. Your buyer must take personal delivery.

➤ *Relationships:* While some computer makers sell their products directly to users, all car makers have established dealer channels that must be dealt with in selling online. While some homes are sold directly, most transactions take place through realtors, and most realty listings protect the listing agent from having the property sold outside that system.

While all these concerns are real, they can be overcome with time, patience, and money. To sell a big-ticket item online, you're going to need some financial wherewithal. You have to finance your inventory, if you're a car lot, or establish some relationship with someone else who's financing a car lot.

You have to offer some financing options, and the quality of those options will help determine how much business you can win. You must have real business links (as opposed to virtual, Internet hyperlinks) to the people who have cars, houses, and money for sale, if you're to act as an intermediary between buyers and sellers. Or you need to already be a large car dealer or realtor before going into the business. Another way to look at these problems is to see them as opportunities—separate niches waiting to be exploited. Just as in the real world, you may specialize geographically, or you could specialize in a specific auto or service within your chosen niche.

In the automobile area, you could offer financing in a given geographic area or specialize in classic used cars. In the real estate area, you could offer financing or local listings, or specialize in commercial or residential listings. While the Internet is a worldwide network, the complexity of selling big-ticket items makes it easier for a local business to do business in its local area. Here are just two of hundreds of examples we found, Web pages for real businesses that expand the owners' marketing reach:

➤ *Best Buy Repo* (www.12go.com/bestbuy.htm), which resells repossessed cars for banks, offers its inventory in a text format and puts the name and phone number of the owner at the bottom of the page.

➤ *AutoSearch USA* (www.autosearchusa.com) is a resource for a half dozen car dealers in Orange County, California.

In the real estate industry, listings, or offers to sell, are a valuable commodity in their own right, and a database of such listings can be, by itself, a good business, even if the site operator isn't directly selling the product.

That's the theory behind Homenet (www.homenet.com), a database-driven site based in Ft. Lauderdale, Florida, with pages sponsored by mortgage brokers, real estate agencies, and other players in the market. Real estate agents who subscribe to Homenet's services can offer full-page listings on properties, linked to the home pages of individual agents. Those pages, in turn, can show all the agent's listings, and offer space for a biography and some philosophy. By offering its database of listings and financing through links, Homenet has carved out a valuable niche for itself. But it's a Web niche, not a real estate niche.

There are many companies in this Web niche. Some, like Homenet, specialize in real estate. Others, like National InterAd (www.nia.com), have listings in many categories, from homes to yachts to used cars, and great expectations of expanding into other niches—NIA wants to compete with Microsoft's Sidewalk (www.seattle.sidewalk.com) site in its home turf. NIA also runs a similar site called HomeScout (www.homescout.com)—there's no reason why you can't have more than one piece on this board.

There is no doubt that the buyers are there. The National Association of Automobile Dealers (www.nadanet.com) released a survey of its members in October 1997 indicating the average dealer with a Web site sold five cars a month with help from that site—plenty of traffic to justify the expense. The same survey indicated those with used-car lots didn't fare as well, with an average of just three car sales per month, and lower priced cars to boot.

About half of all new car dealers surveyed had Web sites, the survey revealed, and another 40 percent planned to launch sites within six months. The Web-based dealers are also becoming increasingly savvy; according to the survey, almost half said they planned significant upgrades in the next six months.

The sales are there, and there's still time to get in the game. In the race to sell big-ticket items on the Web, you have many choices. You can, like Homenet, seek a Web niche. You may, as with AutoSearch, exploit a real niche, expanding your real business. Or you may choose to combine the two. Following is a look at how some actual Internet sites and product manufacturers are succeeding in selling big-ticket items online.

■ WHAT ARE BUYERS LIKE?

With the growing volume of Internet-based car and home buying, there's a great deal of interest in who these people are. In July 1997, *Forbes* magazine published a survey on how "Internet Savvy" car buyers were (www.forbes.com /tool/html/97/july/angles0723/savvy.htm). In general, the survey found the most popular car among the Net savvy was Volkswagen, while Land Rovers were favored on the high-end of the market. Volkswagen it seems, has a very active newsgroup (www.rec.auto.vw) where the cars are discussed in a civil atmosphere. Yahoo lists three chat links on GeoCities, America Online, and the Classic Cars (www.classicars.com) site devoted to Volkswagen. Volkswagen's own Web site, on the other hand, is not very extensive. The reverse is true of Saturn—its buyers were least Net savvy, on average, yet the company has a very extensive Web presence (www.saturn.com), that lets potential buyers configure and price cars online (the company's dealer network allows no haggling). There is also a Web-based group which discusses the Saturn (www2.uic.edu/~hlee12/saturn.html).

■ FINANCING

There are three ways to handle financing issues. You can provide links to banks or other lenders. You can offer your own financing. Or you can provide a combination of the two, with applications available for submission to a trusted financial partner available online, and links to other lending sources.

Carsource (www.carsource.net), a Louisville, Kentucky, used-car dealer with a large Web site, offers a framed financing page that mentions a number of lenders but actually leads users to a toll-free number which takes loan applications.

Auto-By-Tel, on the other hand, created its own database to analyze loan applications and link the results to major finance companies. The company makes money from the referrals, but it provides value beyond that by analyzing the applications. While it's not a financing company itself, the links and analysis provide customers with the "look and feel" of one-stop shopping.

There is a valid alternative to this approach in offering an exclusive to a large loan provider. That's the strategy of AutoWeb.Com (www.autoweb.com), Santa Clara, California, which signed just such an arrangement in August 1997 with the Bank of America (www.bankamerica.com). Providing a link between forms created on AutoWeb and an instant-approval process at Bank of America's site will take time to create, but AutoWeb is already advertising the link heavily.

Excite (www.excite.com) lists some of the major auto financing sites. These include CarFinance.Com (www.carfinance.com/fin), which does business in 31 states and is run by Barnett Bank (now being purchased by NationsBank); AIG (www.aig.com), which works with Auto-By-Tel; and GMAC Financial Services (www.gmacfs.com), which is owned by General Motors (GM). The GM site links mainly to GM dealers. Delivering buyers to these sites for financing may not bring you money directly (you might track the links and follow up with the companies directly), but it could prove a valuable service which will increase your sales.

If you are doing business within a state or local area, it may also pay to seek links to local financing sources—banks and loan brokers whose officers you know and trust. Generally, any help you can provide buyers in securing financing on their purchases will come back to you in sales.

Home finance is even more organized online than car financing. Sites such as Mortgage.Net (www.mortgage-net.com) advertise online heavily and provide links to a number of mortgage companies. The site is organized based on state, since such companies are always state licensed. The directory for Georgia alone lists over 20 mortgage brokers, all with Web sites, where homebuyers can fill out financial forms and begin a mortgage-buying process.

■ INSURANCE

Generally, insurance questions are best handled through links, but there are a number of options. You may link directly to a single trusted source with which you have a financial relationship. You could link to an insurance inter-mediary—a Web site that specializes in selling insurance for a variety of companies. Or you may offer a page of links to every online insurance broker or agent you can find.

Unless you're a multibillion dollar company, it will be impossible for you to offer your own insurance directly on-line. Insurance rates vary widely. Both agents and companies must be licensed separately in each state where they do busi-ness. If you're selling cars, you may be able to provide a link to a direct insurance seller like Geico (www.geico.com) or AIG, but you shouldn't bring anyone so much valuable busi-ness without some negotiation. On the other hand, limiting your users to a single source for insurance may limit your business—buyers who don't want to deal with the seller you select may hold off on purchases, and subsequently purchase somewhere else.

In addition to these company-owned sites, there are a number of sites that aggregate the offerings of several in-surers, like QuickQuote (www.quickquote.com) in Nevada or Quicken's InsureMarket (www.insuremarket.com). Such sites can quickly offer car buyers a quote, from a carrier in their state, which will be very competitive. Providing links to such sites won't bring you money directly, but again they're a valuable service that can expedite the car-buying process.

Consider how Auto-By-Tel handles this issue. It currently provides an exclusive link to a major insurer, AIG, and by handling the creation of forms delivered to the carrier, it can capture value, beyond advertising, in a business where it has no presence. If you can do that, with a local carrier, you can capture some of this value for your local business.

■ TAXES

The taxes people pay when buying a car or home will vary, depending on where they take delivery and where they actually live.

Generally, sales and other taxes are due on a purchase in the state where delivery takes place. This provides a real limit on the geographic reach you can achieve with an online business. State franchise laws prevent most dealers from doing a national business. The single public company in this area, Republic Industries, is actually a holding company for dozens of dealerships around the country, many of whom sell online through Auto-By-Tel.

There are two types of taxes that car buyers must generally consider, sales taxes and property taxes. Sales taxes are due in the location where the car is purchased, and some dealers over the years have actually invested millions in moving their locations to towns with slightly lower tax rates. Property taxes are paid in the location where the buyer lives. Dealers pay property taxes on their inventories as of the first of the year (in most locations), leading to many Christmas-time sales.

In the real estate business, tax calculations can be a valuable service for an agent's Web site. An example of such a calculator can be found at the site of Oshman Real Estate on Cape Cod, in Falmouth, Massachusetts (www.capegroup.com /calc.htm). While users complete a simple form which can calculate the monthly tax bill on a 30-year mortgage, those with sound cards can hear a tinny rendition of Pink Floyd's

"Money." Along with listings, the CapeGroup site also features other information of specific interest to buyers of Cape Cod property, including links to local insurance agents (phone numbers and e-mail mail to: commands), and tips on buying septic systems. Yahoo alone lists 12 real estate tax calculation sites, all of which add these figures to create total mortgage package calculations.

■ DELIVERY CHARGES

Delivery and other dealer charges are one area where the Internet has yet to catch up with the law. Dealers are franchised only within states, and the charges for delivery to other states vary little. In any case, the charges aren't large enough to make shopping delivery charges worthwhile for buyers.

In some cases, the Web does help level the playing field. If a dealer is affiliated with Auto-By-Tel, but its high delivery and dealer-prep charges keep buyers from filling out purchase orders when they see the damages, questions will be asked. In this way, delivery and dealer-prep charges, which were once used to pad the commission and profit statistics, or for bargaining purposes, have been leveled by the Net.

■ PHYSICAL EXAMINATION

People don't buy cars or homes sight unseen. But buyers who use the Internet are unusual in many respects. They want information. They don't want haggling. They don't enjoy bait-and-switch tactics, so a dealer that offers one price on one car online better have that car at that price when the buyers come around.

The same rules that apply to cars apply to homes. Realtors who are honest in their listings have a good chance of doing business. Realtors who aren't won't. There are many newsgroups where these questions are discussed. Dejanews (www.dejanews.com), for instance, lists groups for professionals such as alt.building.realestate and misc.invest.realestate to real-estate specialty sites like alt.realtor.relocation and realtynet, which has subdirectories for a host of areas. Here, agents and brokers let their hair down. You'll see a variety of pitches for realtor-related services, but you'll also find good information on how realtors really feel about their business and their colleagues.

Auto buyers aren't as vocal about their dealers as home-buyers, but you can find notes in the rec.auto directory which refer to dealers, usually negatively.

■ RELATIONSHIPS

There are many different kinds of relationships which must be built in order to create a successful business selling big-ticket items online. Not all of these relationships are financial, however. AutoWeb.Com, for instance, offers a set of forums for car buyers called AutoTalk (www.autoweb.com/autotalk.htm). To ensure the forum will have value, the site posts a warning about its rules upfront, including its right to pull insulting messages. By taking the time to manage discussion groups, however, AutoWeb builds a list of registered users to whom it may send e-mails. These names are also valuable to car makers who want to know what real buyers, and prospective buyers, think about their companies and products.

Like Auto-By-Tel, AutoWeb also provides unbiased information on cars via links—in its case to *Kelley's Blue Book* and the *Car and Driver Buyers' Guide*. The *Car and Driver* link is tracked by the site, a procedure that's simple to implement and extremely valuable. (Simply point the link first to a "virtual page" which logs the user's browser, then passes it to the relevant page on the target site.) The *Blue Book* link leads to a series of pages with forms where potential car sellers can enter details about their cars which, in effect, are combined behind-the-scenes into a single database call on the *Blue Book* (www.kbb.com) site.

All this is important for two reasons. First, the service is valuable, and that value must be tracked in order to develop an ongoing business. Second, AutoWeb uses this service to give buyers some comfort in their new car choices, or in the value of their used cars. Unlike Auto-By-Tel, which operates used-car lots through a network of dealers, AutoWeb operates its own "virtual" lot, based on classified ads posted by sellers at $19.95 each for 30 days. By first telling those sellers what their cars should be worth, they have a better chance of winning that business.

The classified ads also become a database, so instead of paging through ads, potential used-car buyers initiate database calls using forms. This feature, called autofinder, delivers results clearly marked among cars offered by dealers and those offered by other users.

Microsoft's CarPoint (carpoint.msn.com) uses news, specifically a regular column on consumer-oriented automotive news, to draw regular users who'll then use its databases to find the right car for them. The business model is more like that of AutoWeb than Auto-By-Tel. It will work with any dealer, it uses classified ads to move used cars, but it doesn't yet have financing or insurance options. Most features are readily available to Netscape users. All this means that if you're an auto dealer, you have opportunities to draw business over the Internet. You can get a link from CarPoint or AutoWeb without a major financial commitment, but your relationship to Internet customers will still be different than your relationships with customers who just walk in the door. So remember the rules:

- Time is money.
- Arguments are out.
- Service is key.

■ MANUFACTURERS

Makers of both homes and cars are very active online, but none are (as yet) selling their products directly risking their relationships with dealers and realtors in the process. In November 1997, General Motors launched one of the most extensive manufacturers' sites yet. GM BuyPower (www.gmbuypower.com) is designed to support the company's dealers by letting buyers search a database of car models and dealer inventories, then schedule a test drive. The difficulty of providing this service is highlighted by the fact that the site launched with services available only in California, Idaho, Washington, and Oregon. But the existence of the site, its slick look, and GM's commitment to it are proof of opportunity for anyone in the car business who's willing to get serious about selling online.

The site is a follow-on to the success of GM's Saturn (www.saturn.com) nameplate, and the success that division found preselling buyers on its brand, then connecting them to dealers. In all, Yahoo lists 34 sites related to Saturn's parent, General Motors, including separate sites for all of the company's 10 divisions.

But in addition to manufacturers' sites, there are hundreds of sites filled with information and other services for automobile enthusiasts. Many of them sell advertising. Classic Cars (www.classicars.com), which is based in Bellingham, Washington, lists hundreds of sites run by hobbyists, along with 90 discussion groups on various car makes.

■ CARS VS. HOMES

Perhaps it's the price. Perhaps it's the nature of the business—local franchised offices which vary widely in quality. But except for a few niche players like Homenet, HomeScout, and some individual agent offices, real estate remains an underexploited niche online.

The home page of the nation's largest agency chain, Century 21 (www.century21.com), is fairly typical. There's some corporate information, and there's even a database of local offices, but you won't find links to those offices, and you won't find a nationwide database of home listings there. Even the design of the database-delivery pages is at least a year out of date.

Traditionally, the most popular databases in the real estate business were the local Multiple Listing Services. When they were new, in the 1960s, there were real estate offices that advertised "dial your home by computer." They were getting regular refreshes of cards, the output of a computer database, which agents were placing, by hand, into their portfolios of available properties.

MLSs, however, like the real estate agency offices they serve, are essentially local operations. One national database is called MLS-Today (www.mlstoday.com) that lets agents across the country post photos, property information, and other data about listings in their district. This is a business crying out for organization, because listings are the lifeblood of the business, and if they're not widely available they're not much good—at least as long as brokers are protected.

The chain that seems to be doing the most work to get its listings online is ReMax (www.remaxhq.com), which provides home pages for hundreds of its agencies from a single main URL and makes sure those pages get listed properly with search engines. Even ReMax is dependent on its agencies' participation for quality listings, and it's unbalanced.

Some of the homes have complete files which include a grand tour, delivered from the main ReMax database, including pictures taken inside some homes. To get this inside tour, visitors need to register with a phone number and an e-mail address. The tours themselves are a half-dozen photographs taken of various rooms in each property, any of which can be expanded with a mouse click. There's also a photo and complete contact information for the agent. There's some variation in the look-and-feel of various agencies' pages, but they're all fed by the same database.

The problems with this arrangement relate to the nature of the business. Agents and agency offices compete for listings, and you may need to search a number of offices, even of the same agency in the same geographic area, to get a good idea of what's available from the main organization. This is not a technology problem—it's a business problem. But the end result is poor technology, because who wants to spend hours looking for ReMax listings in a single area code?

The business problems of ReMax end up benefiting large, single-office competitors. In the Atlanta market, that means Harry Norman (www.harrynormanrealtors.com). There, a single search within a price range can deliver dozens of "hits" on the company's database. Click on any text listing and you can get a photo of a property, plus additional information. The whole process is easier and faster for buyers to navigate, demonstrating one of the Web's laws of unintended consequences.

The National Association of Realtors (www.realtor.net) has tried to get into the game, and in late 1998, it had over 1 million individual listings in its database, compiled from MLSs around the country. The availability of listings on the realtors' site is based on the willingness of a local MLS provider to offer them, and the frequency with which the MLS provider updates them. A search on an inner-city Atlanta zip code turned up two listings, both woefully overpriced for the market, both fairly old, both from the same realtor. But it's a start.

Obviously there are opportunities here, for aggregating listings, even for searching listings on behalf of clients.

■ CASE STUDY—AUTO-BY-TEL

Auto-By-Tel Inc. (www.Auto-By-Tel.com), Irvine, California, has built its online business by creating its own dealer network, with its own methods of doing business, then using the Web to collect customer leads and funnel them to that network. The result, it says, is a coming revolution in the auto business.

The company was founded by Pete Ellis and John Bedrosian in 1994, moving from the Prodigy online service to the Web in March 1995, and adding a used-car lot a year later. The company also sells auto insurance through a link to the American International Group Inc. (AIG) (www.aig.com), a network of underwriters.

In 1997, Auto-By-Tel handled over 1 million requests to buy cars and was drawing 250,000 new requests per month. Growth accelerated after Auto-By-Tel invested in producing a television ad that ran on the 1997 Super Bowl broadcast, said chief financial officer John Markovich.

The TV ad raised the company's visibility with consumers and dealers and helped recruit new dealers to its network. Markovich said the company has a goal of registering 3,000 dealers, and once that number is reached the value of those dealerships should increase, just as the price of stock exchange seats accelerates with the market's success.

The growth of the site, and the databases it has created, offers a number of additional opportunities. Auto companies have inquired, for instance, about buying access to Auto-By-Tel's databases of consumers' car preferences, as well as buying ads on the site (see Figure 12.1).

How does Auto-By-Tel work? Technically, it's a Local Area Network of Compaq ProLiants running custom software and a commercial SQL database in Irvine, linked to the World Wide Web via a fractional DS-3 line from Sprint. Of the 135 employees, 36 handle the technical details. The computers can handle 50,000 purchase requests per hour, while the data line can handle 45 megabits of data each second.

All this doesn't come cheap. The company held its third equity financing in October 1997, raising $13 million from private sources. "Total investment in the business is $37 million," Markovich said. "The fundamental barrier to entry is the capital required to develop a national brand name, to develop a national distribution network, and to develop the technology itself."

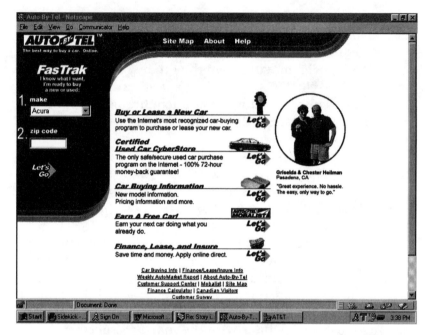

Figure 12.1. Auto-By-Tel provides car buyers with pricing information on new and used models, as well as financing options.

The real secret to the site's success isn't what it does on-line, however, but what it does off-line. That's the Auto-By-Tel dealer network, which closes all the sales generated by the site. Auto-By-Tel has over 2,400 "subscribing" dealers, each with brand and geographic exclusivity. Once it caps the number at 3,000 (out of a total of 22,000 U.S. auto dealers) "consumers will be within 30 minutes of their local Auto-By-Tel," he said.

The dealers pay $2,500 to $4,000, depending on the dealers' location (which impacts the amount of volume they can expect in inquiries) and the price of their cars, to get into the system. Then there's a $2,500 annual renewal fee and monthly fees ranging from $500 to $2,000, plus fees based on the number of customers Auto-By-Tel brings them. It comes to about $60 per car sold, Markovich estimates.

For buyers, Auto-By-Tel offers pictures and data on a wide range of cars, and a simple form they can fill out when they want to make a purchase. The form links to the dealer database, identifying the closest dealer, and delivers a fixed price for that car.

Auto-By-Tel doesn't just sign up dealers, however. It also shows them how to close sales off the Internet leads it generates. The company recommends, for instance, that its dealers establish a separate department for Auto-By-Tel sales, with its own profit-and-loss statement, and a salaried manager whose incentives are based on the number of cars sold, not a percentage of the gross.

The closing ratio, the number of cars actually sold compared to the number of requests, usually rises with experience, but overall it's more than 50 percent. Markovich said the trick is to avoid pressure tactics . . . the experience is more like that of a Saturn dealership.

It may cost $101,500 to sell 100 cars in a conventional system, Markovich added, against $18,500 to process 100 Auto-By-Tel requests. The savings, $830 per car, are split between dealer and buyer—dealers set their own prices—but Markovich says most of it goes to lower the price of the car.

The used-car lot, called Cyberstore, works a bit differently. International Warranty Services of Cleveland was contracted to photograph Auto-By-Tel dealers' used cars and input data on them into the system, charging dealers a fixed fee per car for the listings.

Using the database, consumers simply fill out a form with the make, model, specifications, and price of a target car, and get a quick match from within the geographic area they've selected. As with the new cars, it's a fixed-price deal, but Auto-By-Tel sweetens that with the offer of a money-back guarantee and 90-day national warranty through the Cyberstore network.

All this creates synergies Auto-By-Tel is just starting to leverage. The company has bought a firm called Dealersites .Com, which specializes in putting regular auto dealers online.

That company is building sites for current Auto-By-Tel dealers, and will then seek to do business with other dealers.

Insurance represents another opportunity. Auto-By-Tel has worked out an arrangement with AIG, a large auto insurer, to push its policies through a link from the Auto-By-Tel home page. That link goes to a specific page on the AIG site, a text-based page in which Auto-By-Tel recommends the company. That page, in turn, links to an FAQ file on AIG auto insurance, and a form through which auto buyers can complete a form for insurance quotes.

Markovich said that buyers who come in via the Internet are very hungry for unbiased information, so instead of just offering links to car makers, the Auto-By-Tel site offers links to a number of auto information providers. These include AutoSite (www.autosite.com), Edmunds (www.edmund.com), and IntelliChoice (www.intellichoice.com). Auto-By-Tel also offers its own free weekly newsletter on the auto market. These are reciprocal links—the information sites have links on their home pages back to Auto-By-Tel. This not only feeds users to the Auto-By-Tel site, but also enhances the site's reputation. The IntelliChoice link leads to a separate site created especially for those who come in from Auto-By-Tel.

For financing, the company has created Auto-By-Tel Acceptance Corp., which handles loan applications on behalf of four major lenders whose logos are on its financing page. This form supports the rest of the company's business—it can't be completed until you have a purchase request number, which a dealer is trying to fulfill. The lenders who were part of this program in 1997 were GE Capital, Chase Manhattan, KeyCorp, and Triad Financial. The site can match incoming applications against the needs and requirements of financing companies, passing along matches for processing.

What about the site's future? "The way car commerce works is, we're just processing referrals to the existing dealership network," Markovich said. "Because of the way state franchise laws are written, you must go through a dealership" to sell a car. For that reason, "it's very important for our positioning that our site be considered an independent source of information. While it may make sense to have some degree of linkage," say to the sites of major car manufacturers, "we want to make sure we don't have something that impacts the objective nature of why consumers come to our site."

How about competition? It's there, Markovich admitted. Competition's coming from small entrepreneurs and CUC International Inc., a major online retailer whose program is called AutoVantage. In addition, Cox Enterprises' Manheim Auctions recently launched a site for selling used cars at www.autoconnect.com. What about Republic Group, the Wayne Huizenga-backed company that is buying dozens of dealerships around the country and building a chain of fixed-price used-car lots?

"We're not buying bricks and mortar, or inventory, or personnel, or receivables," replied Markovich. "We're not paying multiples on book values that never existed until last year or so. We're not tying ourselves to specific manufacturers or geographic areas." Some Auto-By-Tel subscribers have been bought by Republic, however, and those dealerships have kept their relationships to Auto-By-Tel. "We believe it's probably complementary . . . we've been told by analysts it's complementary."

Part IV
Cashing In on Web Commerce

Personalization: Marketing to One

The World Wide Web is not a mass medium. It is a personal medium. Unlike television, radio, or newspapers, which are delivered once and experienced in the same way by millions of viewers, listeners, or readers, the Web is delivered continuously and experienced in a different way by everyone who visits your site.

The best way to take advantage of this is by personalizing the experience of individual users. Instead of giving everyone the same home page, in other words, give regular visitors their own, custom-tailored view of your content or your product offerings.

How do you do that? The best way is by convincing people to give you information about themselves and their habits, then run that information through a database. This makes every visit by a repeat visitor a database query. It's a major, expensive transformation for your Web site. But if you can make it work, both socially and technically, it can lock in your customers and provide long-term growth.

■ HOW DOES IT WORK?

There are four ways to add personalization to your Web site. Let's review them.

■ KEYWORDS

The easiest way to personalize a user's view of your site is with keywords. You can see keyword-based customization at many popular content sites on the Web, including Yahoo (www.my.yahoo.com), Excite (www.my.excite.com), and CNN (www.customnews.cnn.com). In keyword-based customization, users are presented with categories of information, and subcategories of information. After they register, they click on categories, and are then presented with the information within those categories on future sign ups. When you have a lot of information available, this is a good way to deliver a personal experience without a lot of expense. If, that is, your site is based on a database.

The delivery of information from a keyword system is fairly straightforward. A user inputs a user name and password, which is then matched to a list of keywords input previously. The data connected to those preferences is then drawn, on-the-fly, through a template that inserts HTML codes for headlines and subheads. In the case of Customnews, which is based on the Oracle Universal Server, graphic information can be made part of the database—so a picture of the president can be inserted over a story that originates at the White House. This does slow down the delivery of pages and raises system overhead, however.

■ COLLABORATIVE FILTERING

Collaborative filtering systems, such as Firefly (www.firefly .com), NetPerceptions (www.netperceptions.com), Likeminds (www.likeminds.com), and Wisewire (www.wisewire.com) compare the input of many users to come up with recommendations. To do this, collaborative filtering systems start with a database, just like the keyword systems. But that user database must be more extensive than in the keyword-based system. It should include demographic information—age, sex, race, education, and economic status. It must also include detailed preferences, input by the user, which can then be matched against other sets of preferences input by other users. These could be a collection of movie ratings or favorite albums.

When users hit the server, their preferences are matched against other preference profiles in the user database. The preferences may also be matched against the demographic data. The more profiles in the database, and the more details in the profile, the more accurate is the resulting output—a movie, album, or Web site the user might find interesting.

Collaborative filtering systems are expensive. The software itself could cost $25,000 to $50,000. Extensive customization may be required. For this reason, Wisewire decided in 1997 to begin offering collaborative filtering as a service, at $900/month for five sets of files or wires. Calls requiring the input or use of preference information are funneled to Wisewire's server, which provides the output through your server.

A second obstacle with collaborative filtering is that the more detailed the preference data you input on a specific user, the more precise your recommendations can be. But no one wants to spend a lot of time on a Web site reviewing books or movies. For that reason, some personalization vendors are adding other personalization techniques to their software, enabling Web site clients to offer recommendations more quickly.

There's a third problem with collaborative filtering. You need a lot of information from a lot of people to make useful recommendations. For that reason, Firefly joined with Netscape, Microsoft, and other companies in mid-1997 to support an Open Profiling Standard that not only provides a common format for such information, but a system of rules giving users control over the information they give Web sites.

You can find examples of collaborative filtering systems in action at sites like Barnes & Noble (www.barnesandnoble.com), Cinemax (www.rw.cinemax.com/critic), and E! Online's MovieFinder (www.moviefinder.com).

■ RULES-BASED PERSONALIZATION

Rules-based personalization systems like those offered by Broadvision (www.broadvision.com), IntelliWeb from Micromass (www.micromass.com), and MultiLogic (www.multilogic.com) take a different approach to the problem of offering preferences. Instead of matching users' input to the profiles of other users, rules-based systems match that input to a set of rules, or assumptions, about user behavior. If you tell a Web site you're 8 years old and like comedies, for instance, a movie Web site might suggest you watch the movie "Aladdin." If you're 80 years old and express the same preference, on the other hand, you might be offered "Grumpy Old Men."

Rules-based systems have many of the same challenges as collaborative filtering systems. The software is expensive, and takes a lot of time to set up. You need to collect a lot of information from people in order to make valid recommendations. And you don't just input this stuff once, then forget about it—you need to continually refine your rules in order to provide valid input. The software, in other words, takes a lot of tweaking. At least one vendor advises prospects to think of their tool as a process rather than a product, for just this reason.

You can find examples of rules-based filtering systems in action at sites like Fingerhut's Andy's Garage (www.andysgarage.com), Sentry Associates (www.sentryassociates.com), and Kodak's Picture Network (www.kodakpicturenetwork.com).

■ CASE-BASED PERSONALIZATION

Case-based personalization systems, like those from Bright-ware (www.brightware.com), Autonomy (www.agentware .com), Open Sesame (www.opensesame.com), and Person-aLogic (www.personalogic.com) take yet another approach to the problem of personalization. While collaborative filtering tools compare matrices of user input to one another, and rules-based tools compare user input to a set of assumptions, case-based tools can translate free-form user input into questions that your database may be able to answer.

Many of the newest tools in the personalization field are case-based, which means you're dealing with an early code that may contain bugs. You also are going to spend a lot of time creating those initial cases. But you will be able to deliver valid outputs with limited inputs.

While collaborative filtering and rules-based tools can deliver preferences, case-based tools are designed to deliver specific answers to specific questions. They can be used to support buyers of computer hardware and software products, for instance, getting answers from a database of user questions in response to free-form input from new users, so your online help desk can run 24 hours each day with limited personnel. They can also be used to sell auto parts or other large databases of products, for which potential buyers may not have specific product names.

Because these systems are expensive, require extensive customization, and need a lot of user input, PersonaLogic (www.personalogic.com) offers complete system integration systems. The company is willing to host your services on its Web site and to make a deal on the payment for ad revenues or a share of sales.

■ WHOSE DATABASE?

Another new issue in the use of personalization involves whose database, and which database, will be used to create the effect. In collaborative filtering, the individual preferences of many people have to be aggregated into a database that is then queried to deliver answers. In rules-based personalization systems such as Broadvision's, large amounts of data have to be collected in order to come up with coherent rules. This is also true in some case-based systems like Open Sesame's Learn Sesame product.

But what if your goals are more modest? In the case of MultiLogic or Brightware, the goal is only to automate the query-handling process. MultiLogic, in fact, doesn't use a database in its developers' toolkit at all—it uses a spreadsheet. The spreadsheet is used to create cases, and incoming data is then matched against that spreadsheet to create responses. In the case of Brightware, keywords are used to tell software how to handle messages. The result in both cases is that you can deliver value to the site, and its users, very quickly. The question is, is the result a personalized experience for the user, or an easier way of putting users into recognizable boxes for the webmaster?

■ IMPLEMENTATION ISSUES

Implementing personalization systems takes extensive use of several different computer technologies. The technical tools you'll need differ from tool to tool, but most require some combination of some of the following:

➤ C++, for writing cases.
➤ Open Database Connectivity (ODBC), for linking your database to your Web site through the personalization tool.
➤ cgi or perl scripts, for building forms and linking them to your personalization tools.
➤ Application Programming Interface (API) calls, for linking specific portions of your personalization tool to specific user inputs.

➤ Database skills, for adapting your new or existing databases to your personalization tool.

➤ Legacy system knowledge, to link the personalization tool to other parts of your enterprise.

You'll also need extensive knowledge of your Web site's computer hardware and software, along with a lot of HTML coding expertise, in order to implement a personalization solution on your Web site.

What this means is you'll need time to implement a personalization solution. Web sites that have used this technology report that it may take three months to launch such a tool, and that adapting to it can take years. Most of that time may not be spent with the personalization tool itself. E! Online spent only two days working with NetPerceptions' GroupLens, but spent 10 weeks creating its Moviefinder operation.

There are a lot of variables to consider. You need to look at the size of your site, its traffic, where you'll draw data from, and what you'll use the data for. Mainly you have to ask yourself what your Web site is designed to do before implementing a personalization solution. For this reason, many vendors are linking with resellers, and with system integrators like Cambridge Technology Partners (www.ctp.com) to help Web site owners work through these issues.

New players in this space, like Open Sesame, may make claims about a short implementation schedule, or a quick return on your investment. Remember, however, that knowing exactly what you want to do with personalization, and how, may take more time than building a personalization engine. But it's time well spent.

■ CASE STUDY—LOANSHOP

Jack Rodgers is president of American Finance and Investment Inc., Fairfax, Virginia. American Finance is a mortgage broker. The company's business is to take mortgage applications, shop them to companies with money to lend, and give the customer the best deal possible. Its traditional method for doing business was to buy advertising on shows seen by home buyers, then have operators take the applications over the phone through a toll-free number. The business worked, and it grew, but Rodgers saw a big opportunity on the Web. A Web site could be open 24 hours a day. The data in a mortgage application could be on a simple Web form. By supporting SSL encryption, he'd have ample security for mortgage buyers.

The demographics of the Web were also appealing—these were high-income self-starters, just the kind of people he'd always sought as customers. Looking at the cost side of his balance sheet, the decision to go online looked like even more of a no-brainer. As major expenses, he saw sales salaries and toll-free lines. These could be replaced online by a single digital pipe to the Internet, a few people coding the Web site and, perhaps, a professional Web hosting service to amortize the whole thing.

The result of this inspiration was Loanshop (www.loanshop.com), which brought his services to the Web. It was successful. In some ways, too successful. "We were up to 5,000 messages a week," he recalls. Many messages were generic, from students doing papers or from people asking basic questions on rates for mortgages—data which could easily be found on his site or those others.

His solution was Brightware, a case-based personalization tool. "We supplied the domain knowledge base, establishing parameters for how we should respond to different types of messages." It took a month to gather the data, and it took Brightware a month to deliver a personalized system based on that data. Essentially, the resulting solution is a database, and a set of algorithms, to which incoming e-mails are compared, and through which they're sorted.

The results were dramatic. "Some 60 percent of incoming e-mails are now responded to in a completely automated way," he says. Inquiries on average loan rates, or where the company does business, can be responded to immediately, without human intervention. Another 30 percent can be routed directly to phone salespeople, and prioritized based on interest. This is important because the faster a sales rep can respond to a loan query, the more likely it is that the query will become an order, he says. "Our turnaround time for a question on our site was 5.5 hours. Now it's under an hour, and automated responses are out in a minute." These aren't form letters, either. Each response carries the recipient's name and e-mail address, and both question and answer repopulate the Brightware database, "giving us a platform for outbound marketing."

If you know that someone asked about a mortgage rate a month ago, sending them a friendly e-mail asking how things are going, and offering mortgage-shopping services may be seen as a service, not a spam. Thanks in part to Brightware, more than half of American Finance and Investment's business is now done online, instead of by phone. "That's in less than a year, a huge savings which goes straight to the bottom line," says Rodgers.

Once your systems are in place for your Web commerce shop, including sophisticated technology such as personalization, your next step is to start promoting your site. The next chapter will discuss most of the major ways to do this, which will help you drive traffic to your online business and start seeing a return on investment.

Chapter

14

Promoting Your Web Site

The "If you build it, they will come" axiom no longer applies. Sites can invest thousands, hundreds of thousands, or even million of dollars on Web site development. But without campaigns in place to effectively promote sites, even the most compelling commerce sites will have a hard time standing out in the clutter. As the number of Web sites continues to increase, the chances someone will randomly "surf" onto your site dramatically declines. So does the chance they might be directed to you by a search engine. So publicizing your presence on the Web is becoming vital.

In this chapter, we'll discuss many of the ways you can promote your Web site or store. There's a strategy for every budget. We'll start with the cheapest ways of going about the process, then graduate to the more expensive methods. Before you start any publicity or advertising program, make sure you first have enough bandwidth, services, and backup systems in place (including customer and technical support) to handle the traffic you anticipate. If you're selling products online, for example, you want to have a secure order form, but if you're launching a campaign that might draw thousands of buyers, you want to make sure you have a way to process the transactions and orders electronically.

We also recommend you avoid the shortcuts. If you're using e-mail as a publicity tool, don't spam your list. If you're using newsgroups, don't make off-topic comments, or deliver obvious sales pitches. When you work the Web, in other words, make sure you do it on the Web's terms. You always risk goodwill when you go to the market, but that is especially true in an interactive market where it's so easy for someone to flame you for your offer, your product, or your service.

■ E-MAIL

E-mail is perhaps the most controversial online promotion tool, but it can also be one of the most effective. First, let's talk about how to use e-mail effectively. You can respond to queries, and you should offer easy ways for people to make queries throughout your site. If you have separate people handling separate lines of business, or separate kinds of goods, offer their addresses on related pages. You can offer these addresses under names like webmaster@mycompany.com or service@mycompany.com, but if your name is on the door it also makes sense to offer a personal page with a link to your e-mail address. Simply embed the address next to the HTML command mailto, as in mailto:joe.bigg@mycompany.com.

You can also collect the names and e-mail addresses of the people who send you mail. You can categorize these queries in a database. You can answer large numbers of queries in an automated fashion or send e-mails to groups when you get an answer.

You can also offer users the ability to join your mailing list, so that they can receive special offers (bargains, new merchandise, industry updates if you're a service business) when appropriate. Be careful in using this list, however. Make certain you do have an extraordinary, valuable offer or comment to make before sending e-mail to a list, even a list of people who want your e-mail. Also, make sure that it's easy for people to get off your list by sending you reply messages saying simply "unsubscribe" or "remove," and make sure you have a process for handling these removals, and sending a simple confirmation to those who request removal.

This brings us to the issue of spam. Spam is shorthand for unwanted electronic junk mail. Spam exists primarily because it costs no more to send e-mail to 1 million people than to one. All people need is a mailing list and programs with names like "Extractor," which collect e-mail addresses from newsgroups, online services, and Internet Service Providers. These programs are inexpensive and readily available.

And it gets worse. Since many people respond to unwanted e-mails with angry messages or flames, experienced spammers have learned how to route their messages through other mailboxes, often the central e-mail servers of Internet Service Providers. The messages will often include a Web site address where their customers, or suckers if you like, might be able to respond positively to offers, but since the path the message is taking is fraudulent, flames are delivered to the ISP's server, not to the spammer.

Here are some suggestions to cure spam. First, there should be some cost for e-mail. Even a 1 cent charge will force people to pare lists more, while providing Internet Service Providers with new revenue with which to increase their capacity for handling traffic. Second, a U.S. Attorney should read the mail fraud statute and charge a spammer who routes messages through innocent third-parties with mail fraud. It's a low-grade felony, but if someone sends 1 million messages in this way, that's 1 million counts of mail fraud. Once this kind of fraud is halted, e-mail "filters," which allow users to refuse delivery of e-mail from specific addresses or domains, will begin to work, and the flow will begin to ebb.

Until the flow ebbs, however, be very, very careful in how you use e-mail.

■ NEWSGROUPS

The caveats of e-mail go double in newsgroups. Programs that collect addresses for spammers are combining with ignorant flamers to destroy many newsgroups, making some fearful of writing and others disgusted with reading.

There are some groups that want commercial messages. If you have a promotional giveaway to offer, visit alt.consumers.free-stuff. If you've got real bargains to offer, there are a host of conferences with names like alt.forsale and misc.forsale (subdivided by hundreds of types of products, like misc.forsale.computers.pc-specific.portables) where you can make the offer.

The advice here is to keep your message short, keep it to the point of the group, and (if you can) point to a Web site for more information. If you have a bona fide offer, and post it appropriately, you can draw a lot of serious buyers quickly.

You can also take advantage of newsgroups on your industry or subjects related to your industry. With some effort, you can quickly find these groups using a newsgroup search engine such as Dejanews (www.dejanews.com). It works just like Web search engines such as Yahoo! and Excite—input your query in the box and if the answers you get don't conform to the question you thought you asked, change the question slightly.

On industry newsgroups, be respectful at all times. When you address another member of the group, offer specific answers in a friendly manner. When you feel you've been insulted, disagree respectfully and—if you get flamed in response—trust that others will recognize the differences in tone. Whatever you do, don't respond in kind.

Some companies employ people full-time to monitor newsgroups to answer customer complaints, and in doing so can deflect criticism and improve customer service. There are even newsgroups set up for specific companies, such as McDonald's and Nynex. These companies have executives that regularly monitor the newsgroups, and post answers to questions such as, "Do employees really spit in food?"

What should you avoid? Overblown claims will turn people off. This is no place for a hard sell. Making an offer on PC software in a Macintosh newsgroup looks like spamming. Posting the same message to a dozen newsgroups at one time is spamming.

Just as you avoid overblown claims, avoid anger as well. Some people will lie, some people won't listen, some people will write things aimed at provoking you to anger. Don't take the bait.

■ NEWSLETTERS

Newsletters are a great way to advertise your services and your bargains. This is where you can take full advantage of the e-mails that are being sent to your Web site, or those who respond to your own mail and news notes.

Create a short, regular publication. Make it as lively and informative as possible. If you're a store, put your best bargains in your newsletter. If you're a service business, comment on industry news. If you have a publication covering cooking, sewing, or mountain biking, offer tips aimed at helping readers get more enjoyment from their hobbies.

Post these stories on your Web site and mention them on your home page. Set a schedule for updates. It could be daily, weekly, or monthly—and if you plan to add bargains or news alerts on an as-needed basis, say so upfront.

Your aim is to create a valuable service for those who care about the subject you cover. If you sell products, the subject you cover may be getting the best quality and lowest price you can find, or you may offer tips for getting the most out of your product. If you sell services, the subject could be comments on industry news or the news your company is making.

When you have a product users enjoy reading, one you can replicate on a regular schedule, offer it, free. Build an e-mail list. Make sure you have procedures for removing people quickly from that list, just as you add them to your list. Post copies on your Web site with a mail to: for those who want to subscribe.

What makes the difference between a mediocre company newsletter and a great one? Passion, information, and lively writing are among the ingredients. A sense of humor and an attitude (one consistent with your organization's corporate culture) help, too. If your company is known for being serious, in other words, don't launch a humorous newsletter unless you're trying to change the corporate culture. If your company is known for being a fun place to work, don't bog it down with serious corporate news.

You should also take advantage of the Web and its resources. If you see an interesting news story, link to it. If you find a resource like a newsgroup or another newsletter you find especially valuable, then recommend and link to it. If you find a Web site you think your customers might like to visit, link to it and explain why you're doing so.

Be up-front about your goals. Let people know why you're writing them and what you expect to get out of the process.

What are you trying to create? You're trying to create a dialogue with your best customers, or potential customers. You're trying to build mutual trusting relationships that can bring you business when times are tough and expand your reputation when times are good. You're trying, in other words, to build an identity which other people—your potential customers—identify with. You're trying to provide real value to valued customers, turning one-time buyers into regulars.

What are you trying to avoid? Don't make this a constant, overt sales pitch. You'll do better if you first give, then take when goodwill (or sales) are offered to you.

■ PUBLICITY

One of the most effective ways to promote your Web commerce business is through publicity generated by articles in the trade press, newspapers, magazines, or even on radio or television news programs. However, while you may have a great story to tell about your Web business, keep in mind that there are millions (literally) of Internet businesses, with new ones launching or revamping their sites daily, and news editors are bombarded with press releases and story pitches from Web commerce businesses or the public relations companies they hire. There are right and wrong ways to pitch your Web commerce story to the press, and the amount of attention you give to this effort could have significant impact. For example, commerce businesses that garner even a brief mention in respected newspapers, such as *The New York Times* or *The Wall Street Journal* often report immediate sales results (see Shiatsu Shower Mats in Chapter 4).

Writing and distributing press releases is often considered the easiest and most effective way to get press, but with the sheer volume of announcements now being made in the Internet business, it is easy for the message to get lost. In fact, most reporters and editors covering the Internet will admit they don't even read most of the press releases that cross their desks or their e-mail, and some say it's the worst way to try to generate press. The most important thing you can do in trying to reach appropriate reporters and editors with your Web commerce story is to consider the audience they're reaching. If you want to announce in your local newspaper that you've launched a new Web site for your car dealership, in an effort to drive sales, that's different than trying to get an article in a national newspaper or trade publication about your new business-to-business commerce system. It can help to write a press release, if only to provide factual information and clarify your message. Reporters who end up writing a story will appreciate the background material. But do not, by any means, send out mass press release mailings to reporters or editors and expect to get any real results.

The most effective way to reach reporters and editors is to understand the market they cover, what types of stories they write, how to approach them and how to personalize your story. Journalists have different preferences for receiving story pitches. Some, including the author, prefer an e-mail introduction, succinctly describing the news and why it's important to their audience. Others prefer face-to-face meetings and demonstrations. Most hate long story pitches on their voice mail. And all reporters want the story, especially the big story, first. That means if you're first in your niche to create a new model for Web commerce, or have developed what you believe is an innovative way to promote your site, or have a great new advertising campaign—and especially if you are making money online and can talk about how much—tell your story to a reporter. But let the ones you value know about the story before a mass press release mailing hits the wire, and you have a much better chance of generating publicity.

As with all relationships, your relationship with the press must be carefully cultivated and worked. There is information overload in this business, but if you have a compelling story to tell, chances are someone will listen. If this sounds hard, and if your company is of significant size, remember that all this is what PR people get paid to do for a living. Consider hiring one.

■ SEARCH ENGINES

There are dozens of companies that claim they can bring thousands of people to your Web site, for a nominal charge, if you pay them to register your site with big search engines like Yahoo!

While that may have been a valuable service at one time—although there have always been charlatans in this area—the service itself is becoming less valuable over time. That's because there are a lot of search engines, but increasingly the business is consolidating. Once you're on Yahoo!, Excite, InfoSeek, AltaVista, Webcrawler, or Lycos, you've got most of the market covered.

For some services, like Lycos, your registration is automatic with posting your page. You may be able to increase the number of hits on your site by using meta tags, embedding the subjects of your pages at the top of the home page file. Use every possible subject you can think about in your meta tags, but be realistic. If someone reaches your page and finds it nongermane to the subject of their search, you'll lose goodwill. For example, after the death of Princess Diana, many companies embedded their tags with references to "princess" or "Diana" to stack their listings. Goodwill is a very important asset on the Web. Don't abuse it.

Yahoo! is among the few sites you can register on. Click to www.yahoo.com/bin/add and follow the directions. Take the recommendations on the page seriously. Note that new site registrations take time to process, and you won't always be placed in the categories you select. Yahoo! bases its category tree on input from users and its own research, so if you try to pull a fast one you're likely to get caught.

■ CONTESTS

Once you've done all you can to bring people to your Web site without spending money, it's time to consider methods that will cost you money. The first method you should consider is a contest. In a contest, you give something away in exchange for having users register at your site. You can hold contests for regular customers or new visitors. You can run such a contest yourself, or you can contact a company such as Yoyodyne Corp. You can learn all about the company's contest offerings at www.yoyobiz.com.

While a small site may get a good start in life without spending a lot of money drawing in users, Yoyodyne president Seth Godin explains that, for large and established sites, some form of promotion is crucial. "You've got to get past the fact that people are free. Attention costs money. If you're not willing to pay for attention, get out of business. It's not free in the real world." The trick to staying in business, Godin says, is keeping the cost of bringing people to your site below the value you can extract from those users. "Pathfinder (www.pathfinder.com) lost $15–$20 million because it cost too much to set up, it cost too much to get clicks, and there's no feedback loop to get them to come back. That's like trying to run a magazine on just newsstand sales—it doesn't work."

The idea behind Yoyodyne's contests is simple. Think about how much a site would pay to bring one person to their site. Now, multiply it by thousands, and instead of handing out quarters, offer a game where one lucky surfer gets the whole pot as a prize. The least expensive way of drawing visitors with Yoyodyne is a service called Get Rich Click (www.getrichclick.com). The average visitor playing the game there will visit six sites—Yoyodyne's business plan is to make the site interesting enough to increase that average. If you want to be one of those sites, you can get in for just $4,000, which will buy you a minimum of 10,000 user visits. "For 30 cents a person, people can get however many people they want," Godin says. By contrast, most Web banners cost $20 to $30 per thousand page views, if not more, and if 2 percent of those who see an ad click on it (which is the industry average), it's costing $1 to draw each visitor to your site, Godin notes.

In addition to GetRichClick, where Yoyodyne itself is the sponsor, the company also creates individual-sponsored contests. For a minimum fee of $75,000, the company will create and manage a contest that draws people to your site. The company has sponsored hundreds of contests over the years for both large and small companies, Godin says, and has the expertise on its staff to analyze your site and run a contest that will be effective for you. In late 1997, Yoyodyne launched a new contest, called Ezspree (www.ezspree.com), sponsored by American Express, offering a $1 million shopping spree as the grand prize. The contest, designed to take customers to specific Web-based stores, signed up more than 200 sponsors (see Figure 14.1). "We'll follow it up with

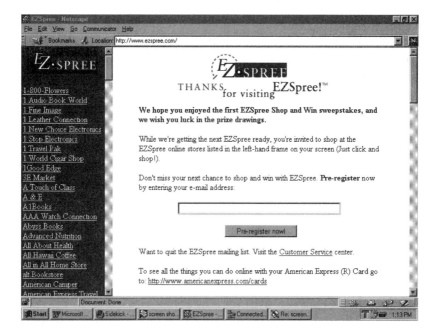

Figure 14.1. In late 1997, Yoyodyne launched a new contest, called Ezspree. Yoyodyne's Ezspree commerce promotion signed up more than 200 merchants and offered a $1 million shopping spree to the winner.

promotions aimed at small businesses, at car buyers, at computer buyers, and there are opportunities to sponsor those," said Godin. Whether you choose to have Yoyodyne run your contest, do it yourself, or find another company to do the job, Godin offers some basic advice:

➤ Have something worth clicking to—a special offer, content that follows-up on the contest, a service people can buy instantly if they're interested.

➤ Find ways to extract value from new visitors to your site and learn how to turn them into repeat visitors. Only then should you pay to draw strangers to you.

■ ADVERTISING

Once you have exhausted the possibilities of e-mail, publicity, and contests, it's time to consider advertising your site. The major format for Web advertising was set in 1994, in the form of the ad banner. It's a small piece of screen real estate, usually at the top of the page, where an advertiser's message is placed above the content. From the beginning, banner ads included hyperlinks to the advertisers' Web sites.

Since those days, things have changed. Some banners have moved to the right side of the screen, some to the left side. Banners are no longer just static files called .gifs—they now include animation, direct response, electronic commerce, and other interactivity. Some sites are using interstitials—full-screen ads that appear as users move between pages. And still others are signing up sponsors for certain areas of their site or integrating a marketer's message into their site's content. Advertisers are learning there are other benefits to banners besides "click-throughs," the process by which a user clicks on a banner to go to the advertiser's site. New ad models, such as cost-per-sale and cost-per-lead, are emerging.

How much should you expect to pay for Web advertising? That depends on what you're selling and the goals of your campaign. Are you trying to build brand awareness, drive traffic to your site, generate leads, or primarily sell products and services? The dominant Web advertising pricing model is based on CPM (loosely translated to cost-per-thousand) impressions, which is the traditional print advertising model. For general interest sites, such as search engines, the going rate is usually $30 to $50 CPM, which is the cost for every 1,000 page views, or impressions, downloaded. However, for more narrowly targeted advertising, such as buying ads on search engine results pages for topics such as "finance" or "pregnancy," or advertising on specialty sites targeted at lawyers or automobile enthusiasts, you can expect to pay from $60 to $100 CPM. Also, using software from companies such as PersonaLogic, you can target to users fitting the demographics for which you are looking, on general interest or specialty sites.

While the CPM model is based on exposure to "eyeballs," which marketers use to build overall brand awareness and drive traffic to their sites, other pricing models reflect paying for action, such as the cost to click on an ad (usually a few cents up to $1), or cost-per-lead or cost-per-sale, in which advertisers pay the Web site a commission on sales generated from users coming to their sites. Some Web sites accept only CPM pricing, while others encourage per-transaction pricing. And more frequently, some kind of hybrid pricing model is used. It depends on the type of business and what's being sold.

How effective is Web advertising? That's what everyone is trying to figure out, from high-tech marketers to traditional advertisers such as Procter & Gamble, which hosted an Internet summit in Cincinnati in August 1998 to get some answers. The biggest obstacle to Web advertising is that traditional advertisers have been trying to equate Internet advertising with other forms of advertising with which they're familiar, such as television commercials, and the media are completely different. With the Internet's ability to highly target specific users and track their activity online, the potential would appear to be huge for Web advertising. But, online penetration is still only about 20 percent, and the demographics of the audience do not reflect the general population, which can be a deterrent to some advertisers. Another obstacle is the lack of standards for measuring Web audience and activity online. There are several competing Web measurement companies, such as MediaMetrix (www.mediametrix.com), RelevantKnowledge (www.relevantknowledge.com), and Net-Ratings (www.netratings.com), and they all have different ways of measuring Web traffic. In addition, Nielsen Media Research was planning to launch a new service to measure Web traffic in the fall of 1998, adding yet another level of competition to the field. With all of these competitors, each measuring Web site traffic and activity differently, marketers often get mixed information on which sites are generating the most traffic, and what the makeup of the audience is. Still, the technology to track Web users is advancing daily, and with all of the targeting and measurement services available, marketers should have a healthy dose of information on which to base their media buy.

The Internet Advertising Bureau (www.iab.net) released a study in October 1997 titled "Online Advertising Effectiveness Study," conducted by research company Mbinteractive, a division of Millward Brown Interactive. The study found that a single exposure to a Web ad could improve brand awareness, communicate attributes of a brand, and increase a consumer's willingness to purchase a particular product, even if he or she didn't click on the banner to reach the advertiser's site. Even a single exposure to a Web ad resulted in an average 30 percent improvement in a user's awareness of the advertiser's campaign and message, the survey found. Consumer loyalty was enhanced an average of 4 percent on all 12 ads tested in the study.

Internet advertising generated $906.5 million in revenue in 1997, according to the IAB's Advertising Revenue Reporting Program, administered by Coopers & Lybrand. And Internet advertising is expected to grow to $4.3 million by 2000, according to Jupiter Communications. Once mainstream advertisers, such as Procter & Gamble, make a commitment to Internet advertising, other traditional advertisers likely are to follow.

■ THE MEDIA CREATION AND BUY

Once you've decided to advertise your Web business, to whom do you turn for help? If you don't have an in-house advertising department, or need additional expertise developing your campaign—or even your site—you might want to turn to a traditional advertising agency or specialized interactive agency. Most of the traditional ad agencies, such as Grey Advertising (www.giworldwide.com), Leo Burnett (www.giantstep.com), Saatchi & Saatchi (www.darwindigital.com), and Ogilvy & Mather (www.ogilvyone.com) have set up interactive groups or divisions, or have acquired specialized interactive shops, to service existing and new clients. And there's a whole new crop of interactive agencies, devoted to new media, springing up around the country. Some of the leading interactive agencies include Modem Media-Poppe Tyson (www.modemmedia.com), CKS Group (www.cks.com), Agency.Com (www.agency.com), and Organic Online (www.organic.com). Agencies can help you create a strategy for your site, develop an advertising campaign, buy media, and track performance.

■ AD PLACEMENT

There are several ways to place your ad. You can contract directly with a Web site publisher, who will place your ads in specific locations on specific sites, using their Web ad server or those of third parties. Some of the leading ad servers and management companies include:

- ➤ AdKnowledge (www.adknowledge.com).
- ➤ Engage Technologies (www.engagetech.com).
- ➤ Imgis (www.imgis.com).
- ➤ MatchLogic (www.matchlogic.com).
- ➤ NetGravity (www.netgravity.com).

Or, you can place your ad through a Web ad network, such as one of the following:

- ➤ DoubleClick (www.doubleclick.net).
- ➤ LinkExchange (www.linkexchange.com).
- ➤ 24/7 Media (www.247media.com).

Web advertising networks represent dozens or hundreds of sites. 24/7 has about a dozen affinity channels (e.g., automotive, entertainment, and news/information), each with top branded sites in each channel. Also, LinkExchange is a cooperative program that offers free Web advertising on more than 200,000 Web sites. One of the largest Web ad networks today is DoubleClick Inc. (www.doubleclick.net), New York. The company not only represents hundreds of U.S. sites—it has formed joint ventures using its technology in Japan, Canada, and the United Kingdom, with more on the way. Among the important Web sites represented by DoubleClick are AltaVista (www.altavista.digital.com), USA Today (www.usatoday.com), and Intuit Inc.'s Quicken Financial Network (www.qfn.com) (see Figure 14.2).

Kevin O'Connor is the president of DoubleClick. "We can sell keywords or content," he says, with keywords being the

Figure 14.2. DoubleClick places ads for clients on hundreds of sites in its network, from narrowly targeted ones to broader search engine sites.

more precise targeting measure. Keywords are not only used on search engines but within many editorial sites. They can also be used for searches within editorial sites.

Precise targeting costs more than imprecise targeting, however. O'Connor also warns that some keywords are more popular than others. "If I'm trying to buy keywords like 'apartments,' they're gone forever. Or the keyword 'books'—you won't find it. You're late to the party. But if I don't care who I reach, and do a run-of-network ad, I can get inventory real cheap."

The difficulty is matching precise targets to inventory, he added. "If someone searches on the words 'Southampton Real Estate' you know what you're looking for, but there are limits on what you can get," how many impressions you can buy with such precise targeting. "With content you're looking more broadly" and may be able to run your ads many times in a short timeframe.

What's this going to cost? DoubleClick runs Web ad campaigns costing as little as $3,000, O'Connor said, although the amount of time they'll spend advising you will increase with the amount of money you're spending. The cost per 1,000 impressions (CPM) of a typical DoubleClick campaign will range from $3 to $100, depending on how narrow the target is and how many impressions are purchased.

What advice could O'Connor offer? "The most important thing to do is test. You have to see which creative offers work the best, and which audiences deliver the best results. Then you need to consider follow through—where you dump the user. If I'm trying to sell flowers, take them to a page where they can do the order, rather than making them wade through all your content. Every time someone has to take a link, you're losing audience."

Customers get more help. There's a password-protected "resource center" on the DoubleClick site where ad buyers can get help on creative ideas as well as placement. The password and account number can also get you up-to-the-minute reports on how your campaign is doing. "You can do queries on our database or download a report," he said.

If your ad is aimed at a direct sale, there are four fundamental variables to consider:

➤ The product, which must be right before the offer is made;

➤ The creative, the ad banner itself, which must urge action;

➤ The audience, making sure your ad is directed to the right people; and

➤ Conversion, close measurement of how many people actually make a purchase, or perform some other action in response to an ad, compared to how many people in your target market see the ad.

While some specific keywords, and ads on some sites, are all sold-out, O'Connor added, there's always more inventory becoming available. It's not all on editorial sites, either. Macromedia (www.macromedia.com) is one of many companies that sell ads on its site—some for completely different products.

While promoting your site can drive traffic, and ultimately new business, to your company, it's important to consider some of the impacts of Web commerce on the traditional sales channel. Some of these issues will be discussed in the next chapter.

Chapter 15

Where's the Middleman?

When the Web was new, in 1994, there were many predictions that it would eliminate the middleman, a process called *disintermediation*. Companies that were already selling their products directly to consumers, using direct mail or toll-free numbers, found they were able to quickly take advantage of the Web's economies and integrate their offerings later. When a product manufacturer like Dell Computer (www.dell.com) or Cisco Systems (www.cisco.com) takes an order online, they save money over the cost of taking that order via a toll-free line and an operator. Once the actual costs of setting up the Web site and stimulating demand through advertising are accounted for, this money flows directly to their bottom line. The same thing happens when a major direct-mail merchant like Insight (www.insight.com), which sells computers and software, uses the Web. We've seen that the costs of handling a form and integrating that form with existing transaction processing and order handling systems, can be much lower than the cost of paying an operator to take the same order. As volumes increase, so do savings.

The Web can eliminate other types of middlemen, too. Before creating Andy's Garage (www.andysgarage.com),

Fingerhut Corp. had to either print catalogs to get rid of excess merchandise, or take a huge hit to profits by selling it to a store specializing in close-outs. The success of the site has not only cleared out Fingerhut's own excess inventory, but given it the opportunity to sell excess inventories of other merchants, and purchase new products for sale exclusively on the Web. It's now a competitor to companies it used to be dependent upon.

The online auction service Onsale (www.onsale.com) finds itself performing a similar function to Andy's Garage. Stores and manufacturers can use Onsale to clear out excess inventory in small quantities and keep some of their retailing profits. The alternative would be to sell in quantity to someone who specializes in selling close-outs. While the sites are clearly very different, we can see that Andy's Garage and Onsale are, on the Web, selling those with close-out products the same service—they're becoming competitors.

■ THE WEB SITE AS MIDDLEMAN

Does this mean the Web eliminates the middleman? No, it does not. It does, however, change the middleman's role. In the industrial era, the middlemen made a living by using their money to buy goods, store goods, and find new buyers. Their profit came from the difference between the amount of money they paid for their merchandise in bulk and what they got from selling it in smaller lots.

Today, the Web site itself is the middleman, providing information to buyers to use in choosing merchandise, and offering sellers access to those buyers. Let's look at some examples:

➤ For stock buyers, sites like Telescan's Wall Street City (www.wallstreetcity.com) offer charts, news, and links to stock brokers.

> ➤ If you buy a lot of insurance, you may want to stay in touch with the Insurance News Network (www.in-sure.com), which provides links to most carriers, daily insurance industry news, and data from both state insurance regulators and private ratings agencies.

> ➤ If you're a writer, a site like Writers Write (www .writerswrite.com) can put you in touch with other writers, as well as publishers and agents.

What do sites like these have in common? They're specialized, for one thing. They know their markets, and the players in those markets.

■ INFORMATION AS INTERMEDIARY

What today's middlemen offer, mainly, is information. They can give buyers an assurance they're getting a good deal. They provide sellers a ready supply of savvy buyers. They facilitate contact between the two, both formally (within the site) and informally (via e-mail and links). They also don't rely solely on their own resources for the value they provide. They use links to connect those in their markets to news, directories, and other sources of information.

In all these cases, information itself is the intermediary between buyers and sellers, and these Web sites win by providing that information.

Before people buy most things, they need information and information comes in many forms. They want to find out what kind of product they want to buy to fill a specific need. They want to know what the competing alternatives are. Finally, they want some assurance they're getting value—they need competitive pricing information.

In the real world, advertising fills much of this first need by stimulating needs and offering products to fill those needs. You have a sweet tooth, you see ads for Oreo cookies, so you go to the grocery store and buy Oreos. Grocers may buy ads aiming to convince you their prices are best on Oreos and other products, but in this case the need and product information were both filled in that first Oreo ad. You need gas, and television ads may convince you to buy a specific brand, but you're most likely to get your pricing information from driving around looking at the signboards outside gas stations.

For more considered purchases, you will demand more information, and when Web sites offer that information, they provide a valuable service that advertisers may pay for. This is where today's information intermediaries excel. They search the Web for news, databases, and actors in their markets' dramas. They act as advocates for both sides in every transaction.

Let's look at some of the types of information sellers can offer, and which Web sites can help provide.

■ BRAND

A brand can be very powerful, for middlemen as well as manufacturers. People buy Coca-Cola, they eat at McDonald's, they drive a Chevrolet. They also shop at Wal-Mart and Costco.

Brands are built from the ground-up. The legendary Coca-Cola Chairman Robert Woodruff recalled that the key moment in building that brand came when he took over the company in the mid-1920s. Rather than tackling a dispute over syrup prices, he asked bottlers how he could work with them to guarantee the product would taste the same no matter where it was purchased. The result was a series of moves to improve quality, so advertising wasn't wasted.

Advertising alone doesn't build brands. You need a quality product or service, and you need to keep your cool in a crisis. (Remember the Tylenol scare? Remember New Coke?) To succeed, a brand message must be attractive, consistent, and ubiquitous.

How can the Web build brand awareness? A 1997 study by Millward Brown Interactive for the Internet Advertising

Bureau (www.iab.net) showed new brands drew large increases in consumer awareness when they advertised on the Web. Exposure to a Web banner, in fact, increased recognition and favorable opinions on new brands even more than exposure to television ads did, according to the study.

How can you take advantage of this in re-selling products or services? Concentrate on the customer, bring them a simple message, and follow through. Information brands like C/Net (www.cnet.com), once established on the Web, also have the ability to create online stores, by trading directly on their credibility. C/Net established several sales outlets for hardware and software based on its news brand, while continuing to take ads for competitors on its site. Among the brands established by C/Net over the past few years are Download.com (www.download.com), BuyDirect.com (www.buydirect.com), and Shareware.com (www.shareware.com).

■ FEATURES

Middlemen, more than manufacturers, must bring new technology to their users, in an easy-to-use way, to succeed online. The bar is always being raised. In 1995, it was enough to have a storefront, written in HTML. In 1996, you needed a cash register that could take orders using SSL encryption. By 1997, you really needed to have inventory, usually in the form of an online database which was easy to search with simple, Yahoo!-like keywords.

For 1998 and beyond, you need an online salesperson. (For more information, see Chapter 13.) You need the ability to size up customers, direct them to the merchandise they want, answer questions, and provide service. This means more than software. It also means fast response to e-mail queries. It can also mean building loyalty with regular contacts, as we'll discuss later in this chapter.

Once you have all this on your Web site, sell it. Use all the marketing tactics available offline. Your Web ads can show bargains, they can offer contests, and they can be pitched directly at your customer. If you're selling business-to-business products, run your campaign on business-to-business sites like Manufacturing.Net (www.manufacturing.net), Grainger.Com (www.grainger.com), or Industry.Net (www.industry.net). You can also use a Web advertising network to help you target your ad. (See Chapter 14 for more ideas.)

Above all, consider what it is you want your ad to motivate people to do. If you're trying to get a direct sale, consider a direct link to an order form and a can't-miss product offer. If you're trying to build awareness of your features, use a link that leads to that feature. You may also consider putting an animation in your banner which demonstrates your feature.

■ PRICE

There are several different ways you can sell price on the Internet. You can offer regular low prices, you can put an item on sale, or you can let the customer determine the price. Here are examples in which each of these approaches is done well:

➤ *Regular low prices:* This is the approach taken by Wal-Mart (www.wal-mart.com). It's done consistently across all media and in all ads. It's also a major feature of the company's Web site. While you won't want to compete directly with Wal-Mart, you can offer regular low prices within a specific niche. That's the idea behind AMP (www.amp.com), a major parts distributor which was one of the first companies of its type to have a full-functioning Web site, including a database inventory and secure online ordering, in 1995.

➤ *Sales prices:* The Wal-Mart site does offer sales items, on the right side of its home page. These are generally impulse items such as the "Tickle Me Elmo" doll that was such a hit in 1996. The left side of the Wal-Mart page carries the main message, with a list of departments, all leading to a separate page of offers. The best way to offer a sale is the old-fashioned way. Buy in bulk, put the price in your ad, and encourage a quick order.

➤ *Customer pricing:* This is the approach of OnSale and its main competitor, Home Shopping Network's First Auction (www.firstauction.com). In this case, the main page features a collection of items available for bid, and the minimum bid the site will take for them. (This allows you to show prices that are 90 percent below retail without having to sell at that price.) If your ads succeed in drawing extensive traffic, you can stimulate multiple bids that will raise the price. If your initial efforts fail to draw extensive bidding, you can do case studies of winning bidders. They'll give you their e-mail address in the order, and if you contact them in that way, you may get a story you can tell on your site.

■ NEWS

All publications are, essentially, middlemen. Their readers are potential buyers. Their advertisers are anxious sellers. Their editorial content should deliver value that gives buyers the confidence to contact the sellers, who then try to complete the sale. The sellers attempt to support these messages in their ads. When done right, the combination of unbiased information and a compelling ad could create a sale. At the very least, the collection of readers and advertisers creates a marketplace.

Publishers that were born on the Web are doing a nice business as information intermediaries. Take a close look at C/Net (www.cnet.com) and its affiliated sites. Sites like Download.com get a place in the C/Net advertising rotation. The sites are listed on major screens, along the left side.

Links are available from reviews directly to the sites that sell the software.

A combination of unbiased information and immediate delivery is also the idea behind Chumbo.com (www.chumbo .com), a software sales site that launched in November 1997. Its president is David Prais, who previously was director of marketing in charge of Gateway 2000's (www.gw2k.com) site. With backing from a major PC software distributor, Merisel, Prais' idea is to combine reviews from ZDNet (www.zdnet .com), the Web site supporting the Ziff-Davis magazines, directly with online ordering. Prais' business plan also includes creating co-branded sites for manufacturers, like Gateway, so they can sell software that works with their hardware, on a site that looks like they created it, and with no risk.

■ DATA

Pricing information is coming to the Web through sites like Whats4Sale (www.whats4sale.com). Whats4Sale provides consumers with a searchable database of sales events at physical stores such as Best Buy, Kmart, Wal-Mart, and Sears. The site seeks to add value with links to product reviews, buyers' guides, manufacturers' Web sites, and store location services on merchants' Web sites. "We have tried to create a useful site for consumers," says President Jeff Homes. The site plans to make its money through advertising, hoping that stores running sales will buy space on the site to advertise them to sale-hungry consumers.

Selling through the use of data is especially important in the business-to-business market. A good example of this approach in action is Aspect Development Inc., Mountain View (www.aspectdv.com). On this site, engineers can learn what chips can substitute for what other chips in their designs. Access to the database is sold, providing direct revenue, but the site managers also deliver news from the industry and links to manufacturers. By creating value for all players in a transaction, then collecting revenue from all sides of the transaction, Aspect Development has created a great middleman site. The company's hard-won credibility has allowed it to branch out into other, non-Web businesses, such as co-sponsoring conferences, and it is earning a solid profit for its shareholders.

■ COMMUNITY AS INTERMEDIARY

A Web-based community can, if done right, quickly build a great franchise that allows its owners to extract revenue from all areas of the chosen marketplace.

A good example of all this can be found at Women.com's Stork Site (www.storksite.com), which launched in 1997 to serve the needs of new parents. The first clear lesson to be found at Stork Site is simple—focus. It's a lesson magazine publishers learned long ago. If you know your readers and focus on their problems, many decisions become automatic. For instance, Stork Site features wallpaper and cartoon-like graphics on its pages, befitting the subject matter and target market.

Next, cover the waterfront. Stork Site takes advantage of every possible Web technology in producing its product. It has regular chats with experts, a "picket fence" where it offers bulletin boards and the ability to create personal lists of online friends (like America Online's "Buddy's List" feature), and "BabyGram," a week-by-week summary of normal infant behavior. The site offers regular Web features like "Ask Tori," a column on pregnancy issues by a registered nurse. There's also a library which is actually a database of questions and answers on parenting issues, as well as an online "zine" of news and commentary.

Next, track the users. To access most of its important services, Stork Site asks that users register, although visitors get plenty of access to get an idea of what's available. This last point is important. Demanding that visitors register is a great way to turn away business. Having visitors buy in, by seeing what's available before registering, results in a registration database of real value.

Staying in touch is important, and Stork Site offers many ways to do that. Users who register can get their own e-mail addresses, with a Storksite.com address, and receive mail directly on the site. The registration process also makes it easier to build that friends list that keeps people coming back. Another way to stay in touch is with regular, valuable e-mail information—keep reading for more information on that.

Now that you've built a targeted audience, you can win targeted advertisements. As Kevin O'Connor of DoubleClick pointed out in Chapter 14, advertising messages that are narrowly targeted can win a higher cost-per-thousand impressions (CPM) from advertisers than less-focused ads. This is a message niche magazines have understood for years, and it's a message that plays well on the Web. Among the early advertisers on Stork Site were *Parents' Magazine,* which pushed its Child's Development Toy Program, and Intuit, which sells its Quicken financial software through the site.

Once you've established your niche, you have a business to run. There are many ways to expand. You can add advertising to your e-mails, you can put in your own store (or sublet access to your site and put in an entire mall). The opportunities are limitless.

Remember, unlike a magazine, a Web site can provide all of a company's marketing services. You can attract an audience, advertise to it, provide unbiased information as well as in-depth sales pitches, handle transactions, perform customer service functions, even provide a feedback loop between old buyers and potential buyers that leads to more, confidence-based buying. When people are happy with the value they've obtained in a transaction—even an information transaction— they become regular buyers. On the Web, that means they become regular users, who'll recommend your site to friends and keep it growing for years to come.

■ MAILING LIST MANAGEMENT

The best way to keep in touch with customers, and potential customers, is through a mailing list. To handle a mailing list, your site manager needs a mailing list manager. This type of program does more than maintain a database of customers who've agreed to take your e-mail and send the mail. It also ages the database, so you can send tickler messages aimed at getting reaction to your posts. A good mailing list management program will also handle bounces—messages that for one reason or another are returned unopened. The program should be able to examine mailing-list addresses for errors, and place addresses that bounce frequently in a special file until the problem is cleared up.

Lists can be very flexible. The simplest form of a list is a newsletter, such as "A Clue . . . to Internet Commerce" (mailto:dana.blankenhorn@att.net) that is sent to a list of subscribers who request it on a schedule, in this case once a week. The mailing list and content should be managed by an editor and the bulk of the traffic is one-way, just as with a paper newsletter.

This is not the only kind of product you can create with a Mailing List Manager program. Here are some others:

➤ Unmoderated lists are simply shared lists of addresses. You send a note to the list and it goes to all members of the list, automatically. This is great for workgroups or projects being handled by people in several companies.

➤ Moderated lists have someone in charge, who not only handles the administrative details, but has some responsibility for keeping the discussion going and handling disputes. A moderated list can also short-stop controversial or off-topic messages, so it's important to have a moderator once people who are strangers to one another get on your list. There's a well-known list on the Vietnam War called V-War that is of this type.

➤ Digest lists take the moderated list one step further. Once you get enough traffic, with enough messages going to your moderator, you'll want to manage the whole process more closely, sending out just highlights of the day's traffic or the week's traffic, to your subscriber list. An example of this type of list is the Online Ads list (www.o-a.com), dealing with topics surrounding advertising on the Internet.

➤ Sponsored lists have short ads at the top of them, much like Web banners except they're text. By putting http:// in the front of a Web address on such a message, you can make that link hot when it's accessed by e-mailers using Netscape 3.0. You can also have the use of such ads tracked by companies like AdNiche (www.adniche.com), which also places ads on high-volume mailing lists.

Best of all, you can get a mailing list management program for free. The best-known "freeware" mailing list manager is called Majordomo (www.greatcircle.com/majordomo). This program does not yet provide bounce management features, but it does everything else you might need done with your mailing list.

The two leading commercial mailing list management programs are GroupMaster from Revnet Inc., Huntsville, Alabama (www.revnet.com) and LISTSERV from L-Soft International Inc., Bethesda, Maryland (www.lsoft.com). LISTSERV has existed for so long its name has almost become a generic term, like Xerox, frequently used to describe related services like newsgroups. Both of these programs offer Web-based interfaces, making it easier for you to handle management of your list and content. Both companies also offer mailing services, so for as little as $49 per month you can have a managed list attached to your site. Revnet even lets you do this through your own URL, and there are third parties like

Audette Media (www.audette-media.com) now entering the business of servicing lists.

Some hints for producing a valuable list for your site include:

➤ *Keep it on the topic:* Make sure all the content on your list relates to the topic at hand.

➤ *Bring in other resources:* Don't forget to link to any interesting news stories you may see on your topic, and encourage other posters to do the same.

➤ *Take the time:* The best list moderators spend some time each day not only going through their in-box and creating digests, but searching for other resources of interest to the list. Some even write their own news stories.

➤ *Be encouraging:* It's important that list moderators take an editorial view, being an advocate for their topic and all their readers. You need to be supportive in all sides of a discussion, until someone angers you continuously to the point where you feel a need to cut them off from the list. That happens sometimes.

➤ *Promote:* You'll want a link to the list, in the form of a mailto: command, on your site's home page. You should also consider making the list the subject of some of your ads.

➤ *Use your signature:* Every e-mail can include a short signature file identifying the person sending the message. This is a short (usually four-line) file that might be a statement of personal philosophy. There's no reason why that signature couldn't include a pitch for your list.

➤ *Collect string:* When you get questions on other sections of your site, try to use them in your mailing list. You'll want to ask permission of the person who asked the question, but even if you lack permission for identifying the questioner, you can address their question and your answer to the group.

> ➤ *Protect your list:* be careful about selling access to your list. It's designed to serve your interests, and unless the message being sent by an advertiser does just that (which is an editorial decision), you risk losing your friends when you rent your list for a quick buck.

> ➤ *For more, join a list:* Great Circle Consulting (www .greatcircle.com), which supports the free Majordomo program, also runs a list for list managers. It's worth joining.

■ CASE STUDY—MULTIMEDIA MARKETING GROUP

John Audette launched his Multimedia Marketing Group Inc. (www.mmgco.com) in Lake Oswego (now it's in Bend, Oregon) in 1995, with the hope of building a promotions agency. The idea was simple, and similar in theory to what large established competitors like BusinessWire (www.businesswire.com) and PR Newswire (www.prnewswire.com) were doing. Technology companies would pay him to distribute their press releases to reporters.

Business wasn't great, but Audette found over time he was getting more and more questions about online marketing in general. His business was online, so that made him an expert. But he didn't feel like an expert—he had as many questions as anyone else. And the questions ranged all over the map—they were much like the questions you had when you picked up this book.

Then, in late 1995, Audette decided to automate his e-mail traffic. The newsgroup he subscribed to on Internet commerce was becoming overloaded, so he launched his own Internet Sales (I-Sales) list. "It was a labor of love, to help people deal with these issues," he said. It was also an advertisement for the services of the Multimedia Marketing Group. It was aimed at people who might use Audette's services for their own publicity.

I-Sales is a daily digest of messages sent to a single address, directed to a list of subscribers. Every day Audette would compile the best messages he'd gotten from his readers into a digest, then send it to the whole list. It was hard work—some days he'd get dozens of messages. Some were in response to other messages, some were asking hard questions, others were delivering answers to questions asked days earlier.

By late 1996, Audette had become an overworked moderator, a key new job title in the digital age. "A moderator is a shit-shield," he says frankly. "The moderator must be passionate about the topic, they must have the discipline to do this every day," and they need many other person-to-person skills that are reflected only in what they type on a screen. Sometimes they have to nudge discussions along, sometimes they have to stimulate discussions, and sometimes they have to put their feet down. Mostly, they have to nurture the threads of thought which subscribers send along, and, to an extent, nurture the people sending them.

Soon Audette had taken on a second list, for users of the LinkExchange (www.linkexchange.com) advertising network. This list, called the Link Exchange Digest, (www .lidigest.com) covered the subject of effective online advertising. Was it such a great leap to begin accepting advertising on this digest? Audette doesn't think so. The ads themselves are simple text messages, placed at the top of the digest. They usually include a hyperlink, so users of Internet mail programs supporting such links simply click and see the advertiser's whole pitch in their Web browsers.

The advertising was wildly successful. "I-Sales has become a profit center," he says. "We're getting paid to do our own marketing! Usually marketing is at least an expense." But as the list grew past 4,000 users, a problem developed. It was taking a lot of time to manually enter new names on the lists, to welcome new users to the group, and to take people off the list on request.

The solution was software. Audette took some time off to research the market for ListServ software, which is led by L-Soft Corp. (www.lsoft.com), whose ListServ product pretty much defines the category. ListServ automatically handles additions to the list when a member sends a message marked "subscribe" in the subject-line, and deletes them when they send a message marked "unsubscribe." They're not alone in the market, however. Audette also found a free program called Majordomo. But the program he chose was GroupMaster from Revnet Inc. (www.revnet .com). Not only does it handle subscribers and unsubscribers, he says, it also handles bounces, when a subscriber's mailbox closes or has some other problem and a message you send to them comes back undelivered, or bounced. "If a message is returned bad a certain number of times it deletes the address from the list," he explains.

That's not all. The software not only sends automatic welcomes to a list, but ticklers, which are sent a few weeks after someone joins, inviting their feedback and opinions. Feedback and opinions are what drive good discussion lists forward, and people generally begin to consider joining the discussion only after a few weeks of reading along. Inviting them in at this point is a great way to nurture discussion, but how could Audette know, from his list alone, who'd joined when? GroupMaster solved the problem.

"You can set up a new list in about 10 minutes," he adds. "It works on a Web interface. It's all graphical and takes you by the hand, walking you through it." It can even put together a daily digest itself if you want—Audette prefers live moderators. It also lets people subscribe to every message posted to a list, instead of just the digest, and tracks everything. By late 1997, the two original lists had over 8,500 subscribers, "which happens to be the target market for MMG."

All this takes a powerful computer, a 200 MHz Pentium processor with 128 megabytes of memory and what's called a "fast-wide" SCSI, for the fastest-possible access to hard drives, running Windows NT. In late 1997, Audette bought such a machine, along with a full license to the GroupMaster software, and began leasing a T-1 line to support it.

Suddenly he had employees. Audette found he needed an assistant, then he needed someone to handle the original press release business. That person in turn found he needed to hire freelance writers to create press releases so he could handle the workload. During the summer of 1997, Audette had one of his new employees research the list business. "We were looking for places to advertise," he remembers. "Having run I-Sales and moderated the Link Exchange Digest, I assumed there was a large discussion list on every topic you could imagine." He was surprised at the result. "We found there are as many as 350,000 lists out there, but only about 70 have enough subscribers to be worth advertising on."

Two new businesses emerged from all this. AdNiche (www.adniche.com) tracks the response on ads placed in e-mail publications. Audette Media (www.audettemedia.com) creates large, sponsored lists. By late November 1997, Audette had launched a half-dozen lists on various topics like travel and Windows software, each with a professional moderator. The company's tag-line is "building real communities in a virtual world."

"I've thought for years that e-mail was the true killer app, and I haven't seen anything to change my mind," he concludes. "You see a lot of newsletters that are one way, but you don't see many discussion lists. I love them because people can participate—they're letters-to-the-editor on steroids. What happens over time is you build a community."

Over time, you can also build a business.

Bringing buyers and sellers together is one of the most promising areas of Web commerce, and many businesses like MMG are capitalizing on this. In the final chapter of this book, we'll take a look at some future developments in Web commerce, and how you can be in position to take advantage of them to grow your online business.

The Future of Web Commerce

In the preceding chapters, we've talked at length about where the Web is today, and how you can find a profitable place on it. We've discussed some of the technology you'll need, as well as the business strategies of companies currently finding success online.

The Web, however, is constantly changing. CMP Media's startup publication *Interactive Age* reported in 1994 that only 75 of the top 1,000 U.S. corporations had a Website, according to its "Hot 1000" index. By 1995, the Web entered its brochureware phase, when companies of all sizes rushed to put their press kits online. That year, the hunt began for new interactive technologies—chat, 3-D, and streaming audio—that would keep users coming back. Also in 1995, large numbers of companies began building Internet-based networks within their companies, behind their firewalls: The "intranet" was born.

In 1996, a large number of commerce solutions came on track, and streaming video solutions were all the rage, from companies such as VXStream, now part of Microsoft, and

Progressive Networks, which first offered just streaming audio and later changed its name to RealNetworks (www .realnetworks.com). The same year saw the development of "push" technologies from companies such as PointCast (www.pointcast.com) and Marimba (www.marimba.com), along with predictions that most people would no longer go to the Web, but have the Web come to them. Also in 1996, the *intranet* craze was replaced by *extranet* frenzy, as companies realized they could link customers, partners, and other constituents to information within their corporate networks, as long as the firewall was secure.

Now, in mid-1998, it's a completely different world. Everyone, it seems, has a URL—even boxers (www.oscardelahoya .com). Terms like "http://" and "www" have entered the common language, and companies of every sort advertise Web addresses in their television commercials, on buses and billboards. The shortage of names has become so acute that new top-level domains are being created, such as .store, and .biz, so companies can be identified by their exact business. Bandwidth constraints are forcing companies that deliver streaming audio and video, as well as push to generate new solutions. Many large companies are now contracting for Virtual Private Networks (VPNs) from Internet Service Providers like Concentric Network (www.concentric.net) so their employees and business partners can be assured of bandwidth, and so security woes can be handled as a service rather than by buying products. This year has also seen the delivery of true industrial-strength solutions in electronic commerce, with many popular Web sites discovering they need separate computers for various functions of their site— registration, page serving, and commerce.

What will the future bring? Visa, Master Card, and major banks are now working with VeriSign, the certificate authority discussed in Chapter 8, to convince millions of consumers they need digital signatures on their browsers to take advantage of this new technology, and major transaction processors are also laying plans for supporting it. SET is a multiyear effort, and its development is relatively easy to predict, although its fate in the market is not so certain. Soon, we'll probably see national television advertising for SET, which may kick-start its deployment.

Here are some other trends and issues that will impact your Web-based businesses into the next century:

■ LEGAL ISSUES

A host of legal concerns are forcing governments to get involved in the online world. Most of the early disputes concerned issues surrounding sexual content and gambling, but many less highly charged controversies are now beginning to emerge, which will have an impact on your content.

➤ *Libel:* What is your liability for libeling someone online? Should it be limited to being responsible for those who visit your site, when your content can be sent via e-mail around the world? This is just one of several questions to be litigated in *Blumenthal vs. Drudge.* Sidney Blumenthal, an official of the Clinton Administration and a former journalist with *Time* magazine, charged Web-based journalist Matt Drudge with libeling his family. Drudge used a rumor he'd gotten from one of Blumenthal's political enemies without attribution, and despite his apology, Blumenthal has promised to make him pay. In addition to suing Drudge, Blumenthal has also sued America Online, which carried the Drudge Report. The result could be an overturning of a case *(Cubby vs. CompuServe)* which absolved online services from liability for content provided by third parties.

➤ *Links:* Should you be required to ask permission before providing a hyperlink on your site, and can someone else force you to take a link down? Total-News (www.totalnews.com) signed an agreement with a number of important content sites—such as MSNBC and Time Inc.'s Pathfinder site, that seems to set that precedent. (Whether it does is open to dispute.) The Ticketmaster ticket-buying service sued Microsoft Network to take down links which went deep inside its ticket purchasing database after negotiations for a paid link broke down. On an island off the coast of Scotland, the *Shetland Times* (www.shetland-times.co.uk) sued its local news rival, the *Shetland News* (www.shetland-news.co.uk), to force it from offering any links to its content.

Some attorneys claim permission should be secured for all links. Mitchell Kamarck of the Beverly Hills law firm of Rosenfeld, Meyer & Susman takes this view—he represented the mother of a female celebrity whose naked image was posted on several Web sites. His argument that copyright law applies to cyberspace is not seriously questioned. Whether that applies to links is open to argument, but that's an argument that seems likely, in time, to end up in court.

➤ *Copyright:* Music publishers like BMI have followed the movie studios in seeking out infringements on their copyright in cyberspace, and ordering those sites taken down. Viacom's Paramount unit was the first, demanding that pictures and other memorabilia be removed from sites run by fans of its *Star Trek* shows as it launched an official site on the Microsoft Network. Now software is available, and used, through which music publishers use spider technology (the same technology used by search engines) to seek out online music, match it to their copyrights, and order offending files taken down.

➤ *Filters:* Will the makers of filtering software have to face liability issues? This question has yet to reach any court, but as more and more schools and libraries start to use filtering programs like Net-Nanny (www.netnanny.com) and CyberPatrol (www.cyberpatrol.com) to protect young users from accessing pornography, the question is certain to come up. One publisher, Tony Bove (www.rockument.com), whose site offers news commentaries, saw that his site was being filtered by CyberPatrol (meaning no one using the software could reach it) because he posted a commentary attacking the Communications Decency Act, which had just been struck down by the Supreme Court. As the use of filters expand, and as more types of sites are filtered, this is certain to become an issue.

➤ *Sales tax:* While legislators have been attempting to pass laws preventing the imposition of sales tax on Internet access, the same will not always be true regarding Internet commerce. For decades, states and local governments have been trying to force collection of sales tax on mail-order companies. Generally, those companies now comply, when they have a "nexus," like a store, in the same town or state as a buyer. (While the argument was originally made that tracking such taxes was overly complex, software has made the question moot.) The states were stymied in their efforts to extend this by the Supreme Court, which ruled a few years ago that Congress must allow the states to charge such taxes before they're imposed, absent some agreement between the merchants and local governments. But states can be persistent. They also have many weapons (audits, investigations, etc.) they can use against people or industries they feel they must fight to protect their interests. In late 1997, a coalition of major mail-order merchants thought it had won agreement with 21 states to allow such collections, but protests from consumers forced them to back off.

Generally, laws that apply in the mail-order business apply in Internet commerce. Transactions done at Web sites are handled just like mail-order transactions. The argument that accounting for thousands of jurisdictions' tax codes is a burden can be handled by implementing the taxation solutions at the processors' side. (They're already accounting for sales taxes on the cost of the transactions themselves—three cents a deal adds up when there are millions of deals done each year.) Some day, your Web site will have to impose sales taxes on all transactions, either by adding it to the total bill or by raising your prices for all and forwarding receipts on-demand.

■ NEW TECHNOLOGY

You should also keep an eye out for new technologies that might force you to change how your Web site looks (to appear current) or that may give you the opportunity to add new features. Here is an example:

➤ *VRML:* Virtual Reality Modeling Language (VRML) files give your Web site the appearance of three dimensions. They allow you to create virtual "worlds" with walls, objects hanging in space, and characters called "avatars" representing individual users. Best of all, VRML files are relatively small, because they're like HTML codes, not bit-maps.

So far, VRML has mainly been used in high-end chat services like The Palace (www.thepalace.com). The Palace links users on many large sites to its VRML software, enabling large events with thousands of users at once. There are many VRML software companies that have been trying for years to make this the successor technology to HTML itself.

One promising company to watch is Cosmo Software (www.cosmosoftware.com), a Silicon Graphics company that focuses on next-generation Web technologies such as VRML, Java, and multi-user interactivity. Cosmos is the developer of Cosmo Worlds, a 3-D VRML authoring environment; Cosmo PageFX, a Web effects studio; and Cosmo Player, a VRML 2.0 viewer. Using Cosmo software, Web merchants can add 3-D effects to their sites, as well as their online ads, creating an interactive environment to draw users and bring them back.

■ HIGH-SPEED DELIVERY OF MULTIMEDIA

The Web as we know it is extremely limited. The biggest reason why: slow speed. With the majority of home users still accessing the Web via dial-up access on 28.8 kilobits-per-second modems, it takes a long time to download graphics and other content-rich features, including audio, video, and 3-D applications. For business-to-consumer electronic commerce operations, this is a problem, particularly when delivering multimedia and entertainment-driven applications. For example, businesses that want to advertise or sell products using video have been very limited in their efforts because of extremely slow download times. This also has been a problem for Web advertising, in trying to convince traditional advertisers that their messages can be effective in a medium that doesn't rely on television-style commercials.

The solution may lie in high-speed access to the Internet over broadband, two-way cable, which will be able to offer speeds of up to 10 megabits per second. While most of the big cable companies, including Tele-Communications Inc. (TCI), Time Warner Cable, and others, are now building networks capable of delivering high-speed Internet access using cable modems, the service is only available in a handful of homes. It probably will be 2003 before these networks reach a mass audience, according to industry estimates. Until then, software companies, network providers, and even content developers are generating solutions to increase the delivery speed of compelling, interactive media over the Internet.

➤ RealNetworks

RealNetworks (www.realnetworks.com), in April 1998, introduced RealSystem G2, which it bills as the "next generation of streaming audio, video, and multimedia experiences." G2 combines audio and video compression technology with a new transport system, enabling higher levels of broadcast quality and reliability over today's networks. Features include the following:

➤ A new music coding system that increases the frequency response of audio by 80 percent for 28.8-modem connections.

➤ New SmartStream transport technology that delivers continuous end-user playback under real-world network conditions.

➤ Two new media types, RealText and RealPix, that enable rich multistream programming to be delivered over typical modem connections.

➤ Macromedia

Macromedia (www.macromedia.com), which develops the popular Flash and Shockwave software multimedia development tools, in May 1998 introduced Flash 3, a design tool for interactive vector graphics and animation on the Web. Flash 3 is an upgrade that lets Web designers create and deliver compelling, interactive content, even over slow modem connections. New features include:

➤ Vector and bitmap transparency.
➤ Animated buttons and menus.
➤ Shape morphing.
➤ Bandwidth profiling.
➤ Stand-alone projectors.

➤ Sprint ION

In May 1998, Spring (www.sprint.com) unveiled the Integrated On-Demand Network (ION), a new communications service that will enable voice, video, Internet, and high-speed data access through a single existing connection to the home. Here's how it will work: Customers will connect their devices at home to an ION communications hub. The hub hooks up to existing home connections and links customers directly with the Sprint Network, providing the following capabilities:

➤ Home videoconferencing.

➤ Adding or removing multiple lines on demand.

➤ Multitasking operations, such as faxing, teleconferencing, and Internet surfing.

➤ Constant connection to LAN-speed network.

ION is expected to be available to consumers in late 1999.

➤ DVD/Web Integration

Computers with digital video disk (DVD) drives, in about 1 million homes today, are expected to be in 15 million homes in 1999, and 50 million homes by 2000, according to Jupiter Communications. With about 4.7 gigabyte storage capacity, DVD disks can hold up to 2 hours of full-motion video on one side. While DVD players let users watch movies and other high-quality video, computers with DVD-ROM drives will give content developers the ability to let users link to the Web and improve their online businesses. For example, in June 1998, Warner Bros. Online (www.warnerbros. com) announced it would partner with HyperLock Technologies (www.hyperlock.com) to deliver a dozen or so episodes of original programming for new and existing television shows on HyperLock's Hyper-DVD. Then, users could "unlock" new programming on the Warner Bros. Web site and engage in interactive activities around the programming. For example, new episodes of popular Warner Bros. television shows, such as "Friends," would be available only to those users with DVDs, and users could enter communities of interest around the show, such as chatting, creating their own storylines, and buying related merchandise. Warner Bros. sees this as a solution to the problem of trying to develop compelling interactive content for a slow-speed Internet world.

These are just a few ways that businesses can use technology to improve Web commerce with consumers. The next section will examine another strategy to make the Internet more efficient for both consumer and business-to-business commerce: Virtual Private Networks.

■ VIRTUAL PRIVATE NETWORKS

Many in the industry expect the development of a second Internet, a business Internet, based on the notion of Virtual Private Networks. A VPN guarantees bandwidth between specific points—you're essentially buying the link. If your call runs within a VPN, you'll get very low "latency"—it will take very little time for a bit to travel between your computer and the Web site, and back.

You can measure latency with a program called ping, still found on some Internet sites—the program sends a bit to a specific site, then puts on the screen the amount of time it took that bit to travel between your computer and the designated site. Ping programs are also used by Internet Service Providers to check how much bandwidth their customers are using—many ISP pricing programs now ping servers every five minutes and average the resulting bandwidth measurements to arrive at a bill.

Many major sites now offer their customers Internet access using VPNs. Intuit's Quicken Financial Network was among the first. Game sites like Engage Online (www .engage.net), requiring low latency for the best game play, have also moved to VPNs. In these cases, the VPNs are actually connected to the whole Internet, and access is controlled by passwords. When a VPN user accesses other Internet sites, they may experience real delays, but those delays will be minimized because the basic link remains relatively clear.

VPNs are commonly used today by large companies for their own intranet access, replacing more expensive leased lines. In these cases, access is more strictly limited. Users may be prevented by firewalls (servers with security software limiting access to computers on either side of them) from going to the public Internet. There may be elaborate filtering programs (like NetNanny) which limit where they can go on the Net—even limiting access to competitors' Web sites. Their use of resources outside the intranet may be monitored, with regular reports sent to top management if a user is found at a game site or an adult-oriented site. In these cases, the acronym VPN fits perfectly. These are, through the use of software, the private networks of the companies paying for them.

The growth of VPNs points the way to a new kind of Internet use, and Internet access. Your site may choose to guarantee user bandwidth, both within a designated area and to the larger Internet, and charge a premium price for it. You may choose to guarantee bandwidth to your site for important customers and business partners, offering them use of your network. You may choose to limit access to the larger Internet through firewalls and a VPN, preventing abuse of your resources by employees and limiting your potential liability.

When you offer access to your customers via a VPN, moreover, you can do more online than you could before. You may offer access to portions of your site that you'd automatically protect from the larger Internet—your security software would identify a call as originating within your network and pass it through. You may be able to offer bandwidth-intensive services, like "push" channels or streaming video, which might be inefficient to offer on today's consumer Internet. You may also be able to protect their e-mail boxes, through filtering software on your server, from the hazards of commercial spam.

As more traffic moves to VPNs, the problems of the public Internet may tend to dissipate. This will enable more sites to offer bandwidth-intensive services. But it will take time for all this to happen.

■ INTERNET IMPROVEMENTS

The growing popularity of the Internet, and its cost-effectiveness for moving all kinds of traffic, including digitized voice traffic, means the world's phone networks are, gradually, becoming Internet networks.

One reason that Internet telephone calls are profitable, yet cost less to make than regular phone calls, is that Internet networks cost less to build than voice networks. All an Internet Service Provider needs to go into business is a bank of modems to take incoming calls, a router linked to a larger ISP's switch, and some software. All an ISP needs to increase capacity is a router or switch with appropriate software on each end of a link, and a leased line between them.

The absolute amount of bandwidth available to the Internet is increasing rapidly, thanks to improvements in the technology used to send traffic over fiber-optic cables. Where fiber cables were thought to be limited to sending on-off signals, with 1s read by equipment on one end of the link as a light turned on and 0s read as the same light source turned off, carriers have discovered the wonders of color. White light can be divided into many different colors—even invisible colors like ultraviolet and infrared—and the presence or absence of these colors, as well as the light itself, can be measured. If you use two colors, the capacity of the fiber is doubled. If you use 10 colors, the bandwidth of the fiber can be increased 10-fold.

Major telephone equipment providers like Lucent Technologies (www.lucent.com) and Newbridge Networks (www.newbridge.com) are also working on other improvements inside the world's Internet networks. They're replacing routers, which must identify and pass along individual packets of data, with switches, so connections can be made more quickly. They're adding more intelligence to these switches so larger blocks of traffic can be routed more quickly. They're increasing the capacity of the fastest-possible lines—the highest-capacity lines available now are MCI's backbone links running at 672 Mbps. Within a few years, backbone links may take traffic at multiple gigabits per second, and the number of such links can be increased with new equipment.

When shopping for an Internet Service Provider, you'll hear a lot about something called *peering*. When networks peer, they agree to free exchanges of traffic. What they need for this is a location, a Network Access Point (NAP), at which this exchange can take place.

Peering has created major bottlenecks on today's public Internet, in part due to the physical limits of the four major Network Access Points (NAPs) through which backbone operators with national operations pass traffic. Companies that could not win access to the four major NAPs—MAE West in San Jose, MAE East near Washington, the Ameritech NAP near Chicago, and the New York NAP operated by Sprint near New York—simply created their own. Companies like Savvis (www.savvis.net) operate VPN service linked to the public Internet via such Private Network Access Points (P-NAPs). They may exchange traffic with only a few major carriers, like UUNet and Sprint, but if those carriers are peering or connected freely, in turn, to the major NAPs, you can quickly offload your traffic and give your own customers faster access to remote Internet resources.

Another way to improve the situation for Web site operators is to collect a lot of Web sites in one place, and offer the best-possible access from that place. That's the idea behind Above.Net (www.above.net), a Web site hosting company based in San Jose, California. Above.Net offers direct peering relationships to every backbone operator, and its software lets it tell its customers exactly where backups are occurring, routing traffic around them quickly. If your site is hosted on such a large "server farm," traffic between your site and other sites may not pass through the Internet at all. Instead, if the other sites are on the same server farm, the links may be carried in a local Ethernet network at 100 Mbps. (In the future, Gigabit Ethernet networks will, on a local basis, improve speeds another 10-fold.)

Besides improving the ability of a single backbone to carry traffic, improving the ability of an NAP to handle transfers of traffic, and increasing the number of NAPs through which peering can take place, there's another major improvement happening in the world of Internet access. Lots of people are getting into the business. According to *Boardwatch* magazine, which publishes a bimonthly "Directory of Internet Service Providers," the number of ISPs in the United States continues to increase—there were 4,000 by last count. While some of the new players are small operations, and others are simply glorified Web site hosting companies, many large phone companies are now entering the Internet access market, often in a big way. AT&T announced its first worldwide backbone service in September 1997. Regional Bell Operating Companies that provide worldwide access through others' network (often the IBM Global Network) are building their own regional backbones, improving access for all within those regions. Existing backbone operators, like MCI, are increasing the capacity of their backbones as fast as they can.

All this points to continuing increases in Internet traffic-carrying capacity. An executive with Cisco Systems (www .cisco.com) recently predicted at a major trade show the amount of Internet capacity will double every year into the foreseeable future. But without a change in its basic economic models, it's unlikely that the bandwidth crunch will ease any time soon.

■ BUILDING COMMUNITIES—A NEW SUCCESS MODEL

What makes the Web different from every other medium that has come before it? While television, newspapers, and even direct mail enable an advertiser to initiate an economic transaction with a customer, the Web allows the entire marketing process to take place in one location.

On the Web, you can use advertising or e-mail to drive traffic to your site or to a specific offer, just as you can on other media. But you can also provide the kind of in-depth information on your Web site found on a brochure. You can link to the kind of unbiased information found in the editorial section of a magazine. Through a mailing list or links to a newsgroup, you can provide the word-of-mouth information people use to make a buying decision. Through links, you can let potential customers comparison-shop, finding out exactly where they can make the best deal. And of course you can do the entire transaction on your Web site, or that of a store linked to you.

But that's not all. You can also provide customer service via e-mail. You can use mailing lists and newsgroups to bring customers together to share problems, and solutions. In other words, the Web can provide your entire marketing lifecycle. Once enough customers are on the Web, your Web site can become your entire marketing effort.

How can you take advantage of these realities and make money in the twenty-first century? Rather than concluding this chapter with a case study, we've decided to offer two scenarios, offering clues to how you'll conduct commerce in the future, and how you can get ready for that future.

■ MODELING YOUR BUYING PROCESS—A CONTENT ANALYSIS

The first step is to model the way you now buy online. By doing this, you can learn exactly how customers might use your Web site in the future. All you need for this exercise is a browser, an HTML editor, and a page that can be linked to the Web. You don't need that page to be on the Web—it could be inside your own word processor. All you need to do to activate this solution is to go online with your local Internet Service Provider, even via modem, then access (and work on) that local page. (Netscape Gold 3.0 is a simple program, available for quick download, which provides everything you need for this exercise. If you have Microsoft Office '97, including the Internet Explorer browser, you also have everything you need to do this exercise. If you don't like Explorer, but you have Netscape Navigator, Word will integrate with it if it doesn't find the other browser.)

The title of this page will be something you want to buy. For fun, you could choose a new suit, a new dress, or a new video system. If you're serious, make it the product or service your company is trying to sell in the marketplace.

Once you have the title, insert subheads identifying every piece of the process by which you would decide exactly what to buy, where to buy it, the purchase itself, and how you'd look for support (biased and unbiased) for that product. Include both the formal processes (going to stores) and the informal processes (talking to co-workers) you'd use in making the purchase.

The result could be something like this:

My New PC:
- Features:
  - What do I need?
  - What's available?
- Brands:
  - Who makes what I've found?
  - What are the specific models?
- Recommendations:
  - What do my friends think?
  - What do the media think?
- Prices:
  - What stores sell this?
  - What are their prices?
  - What are their reputations?
  - Where should I buy this?
- Buying.

- Customer Service:
  - The manufacturer.
  - The store.
  - Friends and other buyers.

Now, turn on your Web browser and start filling this out. What you're creating is a Web page modeling this economic process.

Starting at the top in this example, think about how you'd start determining the features you need and the price you're willing to pay for those features. Search the Web for news stories describing all this. When you find something relevant, insert its location on your sample page as a hyperlink. If you have a link you later decide wasn't helpful, get rid of it. Read the pages you've linked to carefully, going through the buying process.

If you find a graphic, a .gif file or a diagram, which you find helpful, you could link to that page, or you could copy it onto your sample Web page (in the real world you'll get permission for re-printing this information), and provide a link to more information. (You can download a graphic by clicking the right-hand mouse button on any PC while the mouse is over it and saving it to a file. Load this file into a separate subdirectory by your page, called "graphics," then provide a link to that file from your page. It's just like adding any other graphics to a Web page.)

Do you have friends whose opinions you trust anywhere in this process, people you'd talk to before making an important decision? Add a mailto: to your page with their e-mail address down at the bottom of the section. You can do the same thing with newsgroups, or shared lists. Spend as much time completing this page, using the Web and all its resources, as you would if you were buying this product without the Web. Log the time you spend. (If you want to go a little further with this, take a co-worker or employee through the entire process off-line, logging the time they spend talking to people, looking for stores, and checking magazines.)

You will find that in some cases, you're doing regular searches on Yahoo! or some other search engine. Try those same searches on another search engine, like Lycos or Hotbot (www.hotbot.com), to make sure you're getting the best results. Don't forget to consider all the possible sources of information you might need—brainstorm on this with your friend or employee. Most importantly, don't forget to complete the loop. Include links to registration processes, customer service desks, and any newsgroups or lists you may have where you might answer problems with this product once you own it.

What will you have at the end of this process? You'll have a Web page, with numerous links, modeling the economic process involved in buying this particular product. (If you've taken our suggestion and modeled this process off-line, you'll also have a file folder, with whatever level of organization the person who crafted it can bring to the job.) You'll notice that on the Web page, the organization of the information is obvious—everything's in its place. (This might not be true with the file folder.) To see how the Web is changing, renew this process every six months. Do a new search in every area, adding some links and letting others lapse.

If this exercise modeled your purchase of a vacation, you've now got something your whole family can use. If you've modeled the process by which people might buy your product, you've got something your whole company can use.

■ MODELING YOUR BUYING PROCESS— COMPLETING THE CIRCLE

Now that you've gone through your own buying exercise, you've learned some important clues to use in improving your own Web site. Your first clue, hopefully, is your Web media plan. Look at the sources of information you used to buy this product. Consider those sources that actually provided the best service. Aren't those locations where your Web ads should be placed?

Your second clue, hopefully, is your corporate Web strategy. Look at the sources of information you found trustworthy—the mailing lists and newsgroups where you found valid information. Don't you need representation there? If you were able to answer someone's question about your own industry, and got a nice thank you, didn't you actually build goodwill your company can cash in on? Regardless of the size of your company, including marketing staff, isn't this an opportunity?

Finally, this exercise should give you a road map for rebuilding your Web site. The idea is to give buyers, and potential buyers, everything they need to model the purchase, and use, of your own product or service. This is how you build your Web site of the future.

Here are some questions, and suggestions, for helping your staff engage in this process:

➤ *What happens when I meet a competitor?* You will, often. You can, if you like, include only those links that put you in the best light. But look at it from the point of view you took when you became a buyer. Is this service? Does this promote goodwill? Most likely, you'll conclude it does not. If you really think your product or service is the best in its industry, links mentioning competitors favorably should not faze you. If these links do faze you, maybe you need to improve your product, not your marketing.

➤ *What about the news controversies involving our company?* Here's your chance to answer your critics. But don't pretend the critics don't exist—if there are stories you want to refer to that you don't like, link to them alongside your explanation.

➤ *What technologies should I use?* Use what's most appropriate for delivering a real service to a real buyer.

You may find you have training video, or manuals, which you suddenly find use for online. You may also find, when seen through the eyes of a potential buyer, that some of your advertising creativity is a bit over done. You shouldn't treat the Web site as something that will, in one visit, sell your entire company (or its complex products).

➤ *Links can come from anywhere, can't they?* You found that in creating your buying page. Remember that in rebuilding your Web site. Offer links, on every page, leading back to important locations within your site—perhaps through a graphic bar at the top of every page, or a menu on the side.

➤ *Do they have to buy from us?* If you are selling through resellers, distributors, or stores, you may risk relationships by providing commerce on your site. But you can provide links. When creating this links page, remember what it will be used for—for buying. Where possible, link from here to the page where people will actually buy your product. Let your resellers know what you're trying to do for them here, and urge them to provide commerce on their sites. Using this book and other resources (like the links to your resellers you may find) help those resellers out—help them make it easier to sell your product, and they'll sell more of it.

➤ *Service isn't yours alone.* You will want to offer all the customer service you can on your Web site. If you found newsgroups or mailing lists in your buyers' search that were useful, that helped you identify or solve problems, link to them.

➤ *Shared lists are great.* If you provide real service in a mailing sent to regular customers, they'll stay on your list. Always remember whom your mailing serves—the readers. Serve them and they'll serve you.

➤ *Mailto.* The most frustrating problem on many sites is the shortage of links to mailboxes. Not all those links should be to the Webmaster, either. Remember, the faster you can answer a customer's relevant question, the faster you can make a sale. Add mailto links to all your pages, and make sure they're relevant. Also, make sure the people who are taking mail have active mailboxes that are checked often or back-ups (shared mailboxes like customer service are great for this) who'll answer that mail.

If you're a publisher, you want to model your readers' economic process, not your own. If you have a product or service to offer, remember it's your potential customer's economic process you're modeling, not your own. Model everything involved in choosing, buying and supporting your product or service, keep an eye on what everyone else is doing so you can link to it, and your Web site will stay current, no matter how the Web's technology changes.

And the technology will change. As George Colony, the visionary president of Forrester Research, said at the 1997 Forrester Forum in Boston, "The Web is a dead technology. HTML is not alluring, interactive or engaging." What companies need to do to create "immersive experiences" for consumers on the Internet is to develop what Forrester has coined *Transactive Content*—a blending of transactions, interactions, and content. Another way to look at this is to offer the three C's:

- Content.
- Commerce.
- Community.

By offering customers a place to shop, a way to get valuable, useful information about what they're looking for, and a community in which to interact with other buyers and sellers, you can begin to cash in on Web commerce.

Index